SIMPLY THRILLED

By the same author:

Ziggyology

Mozipedia

Songs That Saved Your Life

SIMPLY THRILLED

THE PREPOSTEROUS STORY OF POSTCARD RECORDS

SIMON GODDARD

EBURY PRESS

1 3 5 7 9 10 8 6 4 2

First published in 2014 by Ebury Press, an imprint of Ebury Publishing
A Random House Group company

The Random House Group Limited Reg. No. 954009

Addresses for companies within the Random House Group can be found at www.randomhouse.co.uk

A CIP catalogue record for this book is available from the British Library

The Random House Group Limited supports the Forest Stewardship Council® (FSC®), the leading international forest-certification organisation. Our books carrying the FSC label are printed on FSC®-certified paper. FSC is the only forest-certification scheme supported by the leading environmental organisations, including Greenpeace. Our paper procurement policy can be found at www.randomhouse.co.uk/environment

Designed and set by seagulls.net

Printed and bound in Great Britain by Clays Ltd, St Ives PLC

ISBN 9780091958244

Contents

Foreword

This is the preposterous story of Postcard Records.

Preposterous, because that's how the people involved remembered it. Story, because those same remembrances have been woven together in a dramatic reconstruction. The preposterous story of Postcard Records is a fairy-tale, not a documentary.

A fairy tale, but not necessarily a fantasy. Many people's recollections contradicted one another. Others were clearly distorted, whether by decades of retelling, selective memory or, in rare cases, self-delusion. During the many interviews I conducted for this book, various people – it doesn't matter who – told me the following:

'Whatever anyone says I did, I plead insanity.'

'No, but stick that in. It sounds better.'

'They did what? That's an Edwyn joke, surely?'

'Oh, print the legend! Absolutely. You *have* to.'

Yet when stitched together, all anecdotes still clung to the contours of the same truth. The famous story of Isaac Newton under the apple tree might be a fiction but it helps us remember who Newton was, and what he did. Myths exist for a reason. They are colourless realities translated into the sweet language of romance. So it is with the preposterous story of Postcard Records.

As a story about people making records, this book is about the people more than the records: the large annotated discography section at the end should hopefully satisfy anyone equally interested in both.

The reasons why I wanted to tell this story are numerous: because nobody else had, because nobody else would, because it's a story worth rescuing from its own sock drawer of pop history where it has been mothballed for too long. But mainly because it's a story of pop heroism. The victory of the excluded. Whatever anyone believes Postcard did or didn't achieve, Alan and Edwyn never strayed from that most noble ambition, 'to make art'. The biggest reward for a thing well done is to have done it. Valiant purists, they didn't fail.

To them, to all those involved, and all inspired by their example, I dedicate this humble Scottish play.

Simon Goddard
401 miles south of West Princes Street

'This is the West, sir. When the legend becomes fact, print the legend.'

Maxwell Scott

Prologue

By the time they threw him in the nuthouse he was 63 years old, but everybody had always known poor Louis was crazy. The interminably tragic look on his face. The eyes that rarely if ever flickered with joy. The moping moustache he grew purely to cover the cleft lip, which had blighted his childhood conjuring cruel jeers and bloody fists. His low voice, speaking in a frantic, monotone rush. The way he played piano, witnesses remarking on his 'jerky and nervous' tunes, fingers bayoneting the keys in epileptic rhythm to the mental skewering within. His habit of telling people he'd written an opera, currently in pre-production for the London stage, which existed only in the dress circle of his brain. His frequent whispered asides that he'd managed to harness electricity from the surrounding ether, now pulsing through his bones. His sudden flinches when accompanied on beach walks, screeching that he'd just spotted 'a sea serpent!' close to shore. And his discreet confession to one of his few friends that the spirit of his late wife had since transferred to their cat. Those who crossed his path in later years would excuse themselves in that uniquely embarrassed English fashion and apologise for finding him 'a trifle odd'. They needn't have. Louis Wain was insane.

Doomed from the womb, he was a sickly child, stricken with scarlet fever and waking nightmares that every time he left the house he'd be chased down the street by a giant ball of dark energy. He was ten before his parents dared, in vain, to thrust him through school gates. A habitual truant, he'd wander alone through the city streets, teaching himself the language of industrial machinery, hypnotised by the steam and clang of ships, factories and large artillery. It was only a love of music, for which he possessed no talent, which wooed him back to the classroom. But it was his genius for drawing that kept him there. Place a pencil in his hand and this unhappy, restless cleft-lipped wretch of a child was a phenomenon.

After a hopeless if brief spell trying to make a living as an art teacher, the adult Louis found work in anonymous illustrations and greeting cards. His new career was well timed, just as his father died leaving his mother and five younger sisters entirely dependent on his income. His reaction to this grim domestic burden was to run off and marry the new governess his widowed mother had recently employed, a woman ten scandalous Victorian years his senior. Their bliss was short-lived. The new Mrs Wain died of breast cancer three years later, leaving 26-year-old Louis childless and alone.

Well, no. Not quite alone. He still had his true love. He still had Peter.

Long before he'd convinced himself that his dead wife's soul had voodoo-danced into Peter's furry black and white body, the cat was uppermost in his affections. Their marital home in Hampstead was The Sacred Temple Of Peter in all but name, its walls and dressers decorated with drawings and paintings of his beloved four-pawed companion. His dying wife told him his 'Peter pictures' were his best work. Louis resisted her pleas to sell them, under the illusion he was more of 'a dog artist' until encroaching debt persuaded him to volunteer a first festive feline cartoon for *The Illustrated London News*. His 'Kitten's Christmas Party' was an immediate hit. Whether by luck, fate or the mystic influence of Peter, he had found his destiny, soon to be famous throughout the empire. 'The Cat Artist, Louis Wain.'

His catalogue of cats was infinite, depicting all shapes, colours, breeds and sizes in all manner of amusing anthropomorphic poses: cats playing fiddles and puffing on tubas; promenading pussies in dresses twirling parasols; naughty kittens in high chairs; old monocled moggies smoking pipes and reading newspapers by crackling fires; canoodling lover cats by moonlight; police cats collaring kitten pickpockets; kilted cats skipping highland flings; cats playing cricket, golf and wheelbarrow races; bewigged cat judges sternly instructing cat juries; sleek waitress cats serving afternoon tea to dickey-bowed tabbies; old maid cats; parson cats; painter cats; pianist cats; and entire cat orchestras. There was scarce a late-Victorian or Edwardian child who wouldn't have recognised a Louis Wain cat. A turn-of-the-century publishing infestation, they purred and pranced through newspapers, penny prints, anniversary cards and shelf upon shelf of nursery books.

An unchallenged reputation as the country's most esteemed feline fancier earned him honorary presidency of the National Cat Club and the launch of his own *Louis Wain*'s *Annual* series. The first edition was published in 1901. The same year his youngest sister was certified.

After suffering vivid hallucinations of murder and bloodshed, Marie Wain had started believing she had leprosy, ripping her clothes off in public, in constant need of restraint. She was 30 years old when her family committed her to the asylum where she died over a decade later. Her sisters never spoke of her again. Nor did Louis, who was profoundly more affected by the death of Peter. The love of his life had meowed his last while cradled in his master's hands following, as Louis later claimed, a final intimate conversation.

Still providing for his remaining sisters, the constant demand for new cat pictures, the relentless creative strain and the scarcity of money began to take its toll on an already fragile psyche. He sent illustrations by post to magazines that no longer existed. He tried arranging meetings about an imminent cat show he'd organised at Crystal Palace, it too the feeble figment of a weakening grip on reality. He wasted time and money investing in the manufacturing of ceramic cat models based on queer 'futuristic' designs: the main consignment of these hideous geometric ornaments was mercifully torpedoed crossing the Atlantic during the First World War.

He took solace in another new venture, scheming ways to breed and distribute his own genus of polka-dot cats. The final alarm bell rang for his sisters when he started rearranging the furniture in their Kilburn home on a daily, sometimes hourly, basis. He told them it was because of the spirits in the atmosphere filling him with electric magic. When they questioned him once too often about it he accused them of plotting to kill him, sharing his assassination fears in letters to family friends. After he tried to throw one of them down the stairs, they conceded defeat and called the doctor. He told them what they'd long suspected. That their brother was a nutcase and, for the good of all, was best placed in the care of the Middlesex County Mental Asylum.

The papers were quick to learn that the world famous 'Cat Man' adored by generations of children was now a diagnosed schizophrenic rotting in the pauper ward of a madhouse. The news provoked such a strong public outcry that a relief fund was set up to raise money for his treatment and for the welfare of his dependent sisters. With the support of prominent Wain fans including H. G. Wells, and the intervention of Prime Minister Ramsay MacDonald, Louis was soon transferred to the care of Bethlem Royal, the infamous Bedlam of yore, now located in Beckenham. Delusional but mostly harmless, he continued to draw and paint pictures of cats as his mental health deteriorated. Refusing to wash, he became inseparable from the cloth cap he wore to bed each evening, sometimes pestering nurses to provide him with his favourite drink: 'Bovril and soda.' Left to his own devices he'd happily swig paraffin. After five years in Bedlam, doctors moved him to another asylum outside St Albans where in the twilight of life he took to barking like a dog. He died there, at the age of 78, on 4 July 1939.

The obituaries were rich with sentiment but the world didn't mourn 'The Man Who Drew Cats' for long. Weeks after he was interned in the family plot in Kensal Green Cemetery, the outbreak of war gave folk good cause to forget the sloping signature of Louis Wain. A generation of children once enchanted by his pictures butchered, bombed and missing in action. The long cherished annuals bearing his name incinerated in the drop of a doodlebug. Those that survived relegated to post-war attic gloom, the rag and bone cart or thrown away as unwanted relics of a bygone age. Decade upon decade, obsolete copies of *Merry Times, Happy Hours, Comical Doings, Funny Favourites* and *Pleasures In Pussytown* tumbled like bin-bagged kittens through the second-hand maelstrom, from house clearance to junk yard, charity shop and flea market.

Until one came to land in the jungle of jumble under the railway arches of Shipbank Lane in the city of Glasgow. A needle in a haystack of unloved shoes, suede jackets, cooker rings, broken Dinky cars, saucepans, clock springs, tobacco tins, dolls, mop heads, old postcards, old records and old shellac postcards with 78 rpm grooves of 'Ye Banks And Braes O' Bonnie Doon' etched on pictures of Highland scenery. There the book perched in musty desperation. Japes and jollities like the poem called 'Capers' about three 'wee kittens' kicking up wild halloo and brutal noise to their papa's annoyance. And its accompanying Wain flourish in perfect strokes of black upon white. One kitten on piano. Another tooting a trumpet. And a third bashing a single drum, both beaters raised, as if banging to be heard through this cast-off chaos called Paddy's Market.

BOOM! BOOM! BOOM!

A distress signal seemingly falling on ears deafened by haggling, cackling, swearing, singing and the general din of human existence in the late 1970s.

When somebody's ears did prick up. Somebody whose curious heart skipped to the beat and spied the source of this caterwauling. For here, now, loomed hope. Here loomed the fair hand of fate.

'Hurgh! Hurgh! Hurgh!'

And flicked the book open...

ACT I
UNSURE HOPES

1.

It was scarred, it was swollen, and it used to be a face. Tourists and townsfolk gawped in unsympathetic horror. The pavement cleared in its bobbing and unsteady wake. Fat-armed mothers yanked their children aside, their cornet hands stiffening, their faces frozen mid-lick as they tried to comprehend this pitiful monster. Deaf to all jeers of laughter and disgust it staggered on half alive, finally reaching its threshold of sanctuary, where it knocked, and waited. The soft patter of slippers on carpet. The sharp unclicking of a lock. The creak of a hinge. A moment's silence. And then a gasp, rushing into a moan, hurtling into a scream. A blood-curdling, neighbour-startling scream, which lasted as long as it took Mrs Horne to realise this grazed and ruddy balloon-headed creature was none other than her 17-year-old son.

'*Alan*?'

Yes. It was Alan. Or what was left of him in the four weeks since she'd last seen him, fearing the worst as he headed south, alone, with only naïve dreams rattling in his bespectacled head and an InterRail ticket.

From Dover, he'd taken the crossing to Ostend, heading straight to Vienna, where he wandered through the baroque beauty of the Innere Stadt feverish with Austro-Prussian fantasies of The Thin White Duke.

In Naples, he disembarked at the wrong station, dazed by the city's hysteria over the latest mafia killings, before fleeing northwards to the south of France, collapsing on soft white sands and sleeping the sleep of the not-quite-dead while the harsh Mediterranean sun grilled his face to a crimson agony.

For two hallucinatory days drifting in and out of consciousness he threw his body from train to boat to train to the last bus back towards his bedroom haven. As he climbed off, his knees surrendered, his body flopped forward and his burnt-crumpet face tore open on the gravel surface. The delicate rawness now throbbing with the fresh sting of grit, he dragged himself up and zigzagged home, stumbling through the summertime streets, spurred on by the mocking screech of herring gulls as the reek of grease, cigarettes and the Firth of Clyde blended a perfume of pure nausea within his nostrils.

By the time his mother called the doctor he was prostrate under a blanket, his deep-fried head steaming like a fish supper. In the static silence of pain and misery, his delirium dialled for mental comfort.

'I'm just a fool…'

Miss Diana Ross! The siren of relief inside his smelter-head. Singing away his blues and blisters, his one distant chink of light in a tunnel of a life which felt inescapable. A chink of light which now wobbled and fragmented with her approaching silhouette, a blurry mirage drifting towards his bedside, so beautiful and so thin, just like that album cover where, as he'd tell people, she looked like 'a Biafran'. He cried out her name.

'Diana!'

Then he fell into an unconscious abyss, his mind's Dansette ready-stacked to serenade the blackness. Its revolution begun, the needle dropped and confusion sang its masterpiece. Seventeen years of hurt and hunger called 'The Ballad Of Alan Horne'.

The first verse began in Prestwick, where Elvis Presley's royal rock 'n' roll shoes would scuff British tarmac for the one and only time, and where Alan's lungs expelled their first wanting cry into the world in October 1958. His father had finished the war as a decorated major, settling into a clerical job at the ICI chemical factory in Ardeer, beside the coastal town of Saltcoats where Alan spent his youth being frequently mistaken for a girl. Each innocent 'Whadya want, hen?' nailed shut the coffin of any prospective shipbuilding career. But, by then, young Alan was too fixated with fetlocks to care.

Before Diana sashayed into his life, his first love was horses. He took a weekend job mucking out at the local stables, riding whenever time allowed with his best friend June. How she and he were the envy of all the snooty girls from Troon as, together, they galloped through the fens and spinneys of Ayrshire, shaking their stirrups in giddy dreams of bright rosettes and shiny cups. But the reins of Alan's life lay in the hands of fate's cruel ministers who saw his future anywhere but stood on a podium in triumphant jodhpurs.

Alan was five when he was given his first record, a Christmas present of The Beatles' 'She Loves You', which he had to share with his older brother, along with a pair of Beatles pillowcases. His brother eventually started buying records of his own, one week bringing Val Doonican's 'Ring Of Bright Water' into the house, the next 'Space Oddity' by David Bowie. Alan would sit and listen to the latter's B-side, 'Wild Eyed Boy From Freecloud', the same liquid mystery warming his bones as he'd sometimes feel skating in Paisley as 'A Day Without Love' by the Love Affair blasted through the Tannoy above the ice, or the school trip where he sat on the bus rigid under the shrill influence of 'Chirpy Chirpy Cheep Cheep' in all its ghastly excitement.

And so, with stealthy pace, the secret universe of pop music sucked Alan into its core and shackled him there.

The greatest record in that universe reached the UK number one a few months before his thirteenth birthday. A heart-zinging angel cry of hope and despair, Alan had never known the meaning of bliss until he heard Diana sing 'I'm Still Waiting'.

His uncle took note – 'a bachelor' who that Christmas bought his nephew a box set, *The Motown Story*: five albums' worth of The Sound of Young America's greatest hits with the original artists speaking between the tracks. To hear Smokey talk about the 'young cat' who came up with the tune of 'Tracks Of My Tears', or ten-year-old Michael Jackson describe the time Diana discovered him at a mayor's show in Gary, Indiana. To hear Diana herself ponder how 'people that aren't professional singers sing better because they have that newness in their voice'. Ten sides of more strange intelligence than a boy could reasonably bear. And then came Ziggy.

He already knew Bowie from his brother's 'Space Oddity' single but when the Starman landed to demand the children boogie Alan was first on the floor. He was 14 when he bought his first album from Harris' electrical shop in Saltcoats, a pristine gatefold copy of *Aladdin Sane*. Then his beloved June told him the spare ticket her sister had promised him to see Bowie at Green's Playhouse in Glasgow had been given to one of her friends instead. Young Alan wept his sad bosom empty.

Denied Ziggy, his first concert was the next best thing, Mott The Hoople, whose 'All The Young Dudes' had just dislodged Diana Ross as the greatest disc on Planet Alan.

School was simply a waste of their time and his. Mortar-boarded spectres of a bygone age tried to ram Latin into a young head whose sole purpose in life had become saving enough pennies in a jar to afford the airfare to America to see Bowie's *Diamond Dogs* tour. Juvenile shyness mutated into adolescent nuttiness. They called his mother in to explain Alan's disruptive behaviour in class. He'd already given them all the clues he could when asked to write an essay for English homework and handing in a lengthy appraisal of Lou Reed. Bowie was still the sun, but Lou was the atomic core. Bowie came from outer space, Lou from somewhere infinitely more exotic: New York. His songs were sad, naughty, sexy, lonely, romantic and divine. And his band, his old band, The Velvet Underground, were the greatest to ever draw breath. Bowie said so, and if Bowie said so, young Alan usually agreed.

A lost cause to academia, the week of his higher exams he forewent all cramming to abscond to London to see Bowie at Wembley Empire Pool. Sat in the North Grand Tier, row H, seat 89A, Alan finally understood the purpose of his existence. Watching Buñuel's *Un Chien Andalou* on the big screen, then to witness, in person, the bony wonder of The Thin White Duke, all earthly cares evaporated.

To the relief of Major and Mrs Horne, Alan passed his exams. He told them he was thinking of becoming a vet. In truth, he didn't have any ambitions. Only to flee Saltcoats and never work. University seemed the easiest escape route and he was clever enough to get in, applying for a first-year course including zoology and botany.

In the meantime he took a holiday job at the ICI factory where his father worked. While the nation baked in the hottest July since records began, Alan spent the summer of 1976 in a windowless chemical laboratory testing NSM, a revolutionary 'new smoking material' which, its manufacturers hoped, would one day replace tobacco. There in his cancer bunker he wilted week after week, dreaming of adventure until he'd scraped enough to buy some.

The disco whip-crack of Candi Staton's 'Young Hearts Run Free' spurred Alan on to his European paradise. The Bionic Woman, Elton and Kiki, Demis Roussos, Ruby Flipper, the asphyxiating odour of NSM smoking formula and the blank horizon of Saltcoats now lay behind him. He didn't know what he was looking for, only that he hoped to find it on an InterRail ticket.

'And I'm still waiting...'

* * *

Alan awoke with an ungodly moan, his stinging head pulsing in the silence of his bedroom. It was just him, 17 years old and alone. With his single bed, and his glasses beside it. And his Bush cassette recorder, and some tapes of T. Rex and radio recordings of Alan Freeman's *Story Of Pop*. And his *Motown Story* box set, and his copy of *Aladdin Sane*. And a Wembley Empire Pool ticket stub, and a letter telling him where to enrol on his first day of term for a course he'd no intention of studying.

And the constant scoffing laughter of fate's cruel ministers, echoing from above.

2.

As the poor boy from Saltcoats ached in slumbery agitation, some 30 miles away the sparks which would light his unforeseeably bright future were beginning to flicker.

Two such sparks had already kindled a small fire of friendship since the age of 11. Spark number one, Steven Daly, had spent his childhood flitting from East Kilbride to East Africa, returning to his native Glasgow just in time to finish primary school and meet spark number two, James Kirk: christened so long before anyone had ever heard of the Starship *Enterprise*, the son of a chiropodist ultimately destined to follow in the same insoles. In the 'I'm Still Waiting' autumn of 1971, James and Steven together beamed up to Bearsden Academy, the secondary school in their prissy middle-class Glasgow suburb off the main road heading north in the vague direction of the Trossachs.

The outstretched hand of Ziggy Stardust somehow failed to scratch either child, both preferring the full-throttle yobbery of Slade. Steven started to devour the *NME*, taking his cues from the gospels of Kent and Murray, and blowing his pocket money on Lou Reed's *Rock 'N' Roll Animal* at their command. James had fiddled with the fiddle until he found the means and mains to plug it in, joining his first band as the 13-year-old electric bowman of cape-wearing prog-rock apostles, Entropy, an affliction he cured with The Byrds, The Flying Burrito Brothers and similar antidotes in his older brother's record collection.

At 16, James and Steven were smart, sometimes a little too smart for their own good, but with eyes that wandered dreamily beyond the classroom wall and pulses that quickened with the want of romance and amplified guitars. Two ripe sparks looking for the human bellows to blow their fire into a furnace.

Such a bellows fellow existed, provocatively close. So close that Steven couldn't help but spot him on the school bus, reading a copy of *Melody Maker*.

The bellows was called Edwyn and he was a blazing strange boy in every aspect. Blazingly bright and creative. Blazingly gangly and funny. Blazingly tough in his resolute go-to-blazes fearlessness. A sandy-haired, sensitive soul with a blazingly goofy laugh like a hiccupping sea lion so the world would never forget what a blazing strange boy he was in every aspect. A blazing strange boy minding his own business yet keenly aware he was being watched, even as his eyes pretended to be engrossed in the world's least engrossing story about Emerson, Lake & Palmer on page eleven of that week's *Melody Maker*.

He could sense Steven's bolty-eyed scrutiny even through the newsprint. So when the insult came, Edwyn was braced for it.

'Why are you reading that shit?'

It was the kind of welcome Edwyn had come to expect in Glasgow, the city he had been forced to call 'home' for the past year.

Home, by birth, was Edinburgh, where his parents met at art school in the fifties. Among his mother's student sketchbooks were drawings of local life model and jobbing actor Sean Connery, naked save his regulation 'posing pants'.

His father was a talented painter, a Highland-born Italian Renaissance obsessive who took great pride in his lime green Crimplene safari suit and even greater pride finding a lecturing post in Dundee, dragging the Collins clan with him when Edwyn was only five. Three years of blithely happy childhood passed by, drawing pictures of birds and collecting stamps before his mother bought him a copy of Donovan's top-five hit 'Jennifer Juniper'. A sweet folk froth about a maiden with 'golden flax' trotting on 'a dappled mare' trilled in a dainty yodel over guitar and flute, any academic aspirations for her son were unwittingly incinerated in the two minutes and 40 seconds it took for the needle to spin its life-determining spell.

The meticulously ordered stamp collection was first to suffer as Bowie's 'Starman' call, Bolan's 'Chariot Choogle' and other early seventies sensory epidemics took seed in his newly teenage head. Edwyn's glam passions were matched by a kindred spirit at Dundee's Morgan Academy, a handsome creature called Paul Quinn with a smile that hollered like the 'Hallelujah!' chorus who was to become his schoolyard Bewlay Brother – even if Edwyn's own wardrobe hesitated on the safe precipice of baggy Wranglers and a Harrington jacket.

Foreseeing his destiny in more glittering threads, his private fantasies merged with those of 'Johnny Preston', the future eighties rock god he invented for a short story in the school magazine. Johnny had 'borrowed from Dylan, Elvis and The Beatles but what emerged was substantially his own', only to be exposed in the last paragraph as a 14-year-old dreamer much like himself, pretending to play guitar in his bedroom with an egg-slicer.

Edwyn tried to join his first band, a gang of prog-worshipping longhairs called Onyx, hoping to impress by turning up at the audition with a banjo ukulele. Unwilling to entertain a novel dash of George Formby in their Genesis stew, the Onyx boys turned him homewards where he took refuge and revenge composing in his bedroom, sometimes entertaining his sister, Petra, with songs he'd written about her dolls and teddy bears performed *Top Of The Pops* style in a 'toy town top 20', or stealing plotlines from her romance magazines for soppy ballads.

Frustrated with his father's ukulele he eventually decided to sell his stamp collection and buy a semi-acoustic guitar. Johnny Preston incarnate, his playing improved while his songs grew ever more eccentric. Like 'Marsha Goldstein', his ode about being in love with a Jewish beautician working at the make-up counter of a Manhattan department store. Listening to the second-hand sounds he'd acquired by The Velvet Underground extended the scaffolding of these New York dreams, just as they helped block out the traffic noise of his parents' divorce.

His mother uprooted to Glasgow, where Edwyn's granddad had taught Dirk Bogarde at Allen Glen's School, taking her two children with her and setting up home on the edges of Bearsden. Edwyn's faithful glimmer twin Paul kept in touch, sometimes travelling from Dundee to stay over and see the occasional concert. But he was otherwise alone. Just him and his mother and sister, and their kitten called Mackintosh, which he'd sometimes carry around in his pocket. And a guitar to spur his 'Johnny Preston' daydreams and a copy of his favourite book *The Catcher In The Rye*. And the pair of plastic sandals he'd wear down to Argyle Street, self-consciously staring at his acne in the reflection of the arcade windows, a Buddy Holly badge on his lapel and the copy of *Melody Maker* he was now reading on the school bus to Bearsden Academy. Being insulted.*

'Why are you reading that shit?'

Edwyn looked up from his magazine and saw Steven grinning across the aisle, neatly dressed, like a teenage dad, with his longish hair. 'Down to his arse,' thought Edwyn, who laughed his goofy laugh within.

'Nobody reads that,' taunted Steven. 'The *Maker*'s for hippies. You want to read the *NME*.'

Edwyn blazed. 'Who asked you, anyway?'

'Just saying,' Steven wobbled, the rush of cockiness slipping from his face leaving a long, awkward pause. 'That's a cool badge, by the way,' he added, indicating the Buddy Holly button, groping to make amends.

---

* In a detail unique to James Kirk's alternative version of this story, Steven harassed Edwyn for the even more reprehensible hippy crime of carrying a copy of Rick Wakeman's *Journey To The Centre Of The Earth*.

The cold front of hostility melted away, and with it the inner want of romance and amplified guitars began to dance in Steven's eyes. Edwyn's jigged back at him in joyful recognition.

'I'm Steven,' said Steven.

'I'm Edwyn,' said Edwyn, as the bus trundled on towards Bearsden Academy, sealing their destinies in the few minutes it took to reach the school gates.

3.

The first lesson Alan learned in his first term at university was that however bad he thought life could be, fate's cruel ministers could always make it considerably worse.

His European escapade had been a rash act of late compensation for a life spent in front of the television. But now that he'd savoured the outside world, and borne the sunburnt scars, he wanted to return there.

'There' being anywhere other than Saltcoats, even if it was only 40 minutes up a railway line to Glasgow. He was just old enough to remember the steam trains that first took him there on shopping trips, the smoky journey to the smoky city where the buildings remained spattered by the soot of a hundred years earlier, luxurious shades of blonde and red sandstone buried under thick crusts of ash coughed up by successive family dynasties of Clydebank dragons. But it was better than disintegrating in Saltcoats. Or so he told himself as he unpacked his suitcase in a cheerless West End bedsit the night before registration.

It was only the next day, as he stood frozen in the eye of the academic storm and his bespectacled eyes took stock of his fellow students that a flood of sickness cascaded through his stomach. It wasn't the lack of glamour so much as the lack of youth. Theirs looked as if it had been mummified by facts, embalmed by data and asphyxiated by lack of exposure to Lou Reed. They were five years and ten haircuts before their time, hippies in aspic smelling of corned beef, carbolic and *Tubular Bells*.

Back in his bedsit, a scalded dog in his kennel, Alan stared at the crater in his life where the telly should have been and allowed his misery to ferment.

Days earlier he'd been lost in private fantasies, imagining himself welcomed into the bosom of the beautiful, young and exciting, who knew about Bowie, and Lou, and the inarguable majesty of The Velvet Underground in all their specific epochs.

Or new groups like the adorable Ramones, a three-chord Mount Rushmore of grease, leather and tight denim, whose debut album had come out on American import that summer, sparking GLUE-SNIFF DISC SHOCKER headlines on the front pages of Glasgow's *Evening Times* after a local MP made it his mission to scorch it from the surface of the earth for containing a 94-second celebration of solvent abuse.

Or the bands he'd read about in a concert review in *Sounds* during his InterRail trip. One was called Buzzcocks, whose singer, it said, looked like 'the Boston Strangler' and who, intriguingly, braved a cover of The Troggs' 'I Can't Control Myself'. The other was the Sex Pistols, led by Johnny Rotten, who stubbed cigarettes on his forearm without flinching and tore his shirt up during the encore, and whose outrageous song titles included 'I'm A Lazy Sod' and 'Anarchy In The UK'. All this was happening now, somewhere out there. 'There' being anywhere other than Glasgow.

The campus (and its haircuts) was only half the problem. The city itself was still trying to fight its way out of the late-1960s, all live entertainment at the mercy of the Lord Provost and the council's arcane licensing laws.

There was 'the dancing', discos where you could drink and jive, and spill the wrong pint and be stamped into the southern hemisphere by ubiquitous tribes of neds.

There were pubs like the Burns Howff where you could watch Clyde-built belters like Maggie Bell, or the acid-rock hangover called Chou Pahrot, and their wacky frontman Eggy Beard.

And there was the Apollo, Green's Playhouse as was, where Alan missed Ziggy but first caught Mott. Once in a blue mid-seventies moon you might glimpse Roxy Music between month after month of Showaddywaddy, Nazareth, Jack Jones and Status Quo. But never a Sex Pistols, even though they tried. In late November it was announced their Anarchy In The UK package tour would be thundering into the Apollo that Christmas. The following week the Pistols swore live on London TV, the tabloids exploded, the city fathers felt the tremors in their toupees and the concert was 'banned'.

Except the stark reality of the risk was more depressing than terrifying. Before being cancelled, the Apollo had sold less than a hundred tickets. All the punks in Glasgow could barely fill a double-decker bus.

So weary with these and other social disasters, Alan moved

back home to Saltcoats at the end of term, resigned to a daily commute to Glasgow in the new year, beaten by too many gloomy nights alone in his bedsit. He hadn't missed Saltcoats, nor his parents, only the telly. Which he spent most of that Christmas in front of.

To Major Horne and Mrs Horne, Alan was no different from the directionless soul who'd walked out of the front door three months earlier. On the outside, only a few weeks older. But, inside, a few depressions wiser. A few solitudes tougher. A few thoughts wickeder about an over-abundant world of bores and his calcifying desire to put it to rights.

4.

Had it been a weekday they'd have bunked off school, cocking collective snoots with a Musketeers' cry of, 'Bearsden Academy, be damned!' But, as it was a Saturday, Edwyn, James and Steven caught the lunchtime train from Queen Street Station with snoots uncocked, consciences clear of all truant guilt.

Less than a year after the lightning of Edwyn first struck Steven on the school bus the three had become as inseparable as Ramones. Inspired by the weekly punk-rock dispatches of the London music press, they already imagined themselves the making of Glasgow's teenage equivalent.

Edwyn, with his impressively comprehensive Velvet Underground collection, his mutual love of Boston geek laureate Jonathan Richman & The Modern Lovers and his blazing strangeness, had successfully lured James and Steven away from their previous teenage rock shambles called The Machetes. James had invested in the world's heaviest yet conversely quietest amplifier and a Burns Nu-Sonic guitar, vainly hoping to impress his fellow Machetes with his rendition of David

Bowie's new single, 'Sound And Vision'. They, instead, suggested he take future instruction from the possum-eating redneck rock of a Lynyrd Skynyrd live album. Such were the blunt ambitions of The Machetes, who rightly rusted into oblivion once James and Steven scarpered.

In Edwyn, by contrast, they found a sleek and willowy prophet of fretboard fuzz and vocal frolics, who could sing the New York Dolls' 'Who Are The Mystery Girls?' with a faithful Bowery street-trash twang and who was already writing and recording his own demos at home, exploiting the acoustics of the Collins family bathroom. His first three-chord sherbet fountain was called 'Ready, Get Set, Go!': '*I'll meet you at eleven at the corner café, ready, get set, go!*' James thought the song 'an absolute cracker' and a solid enough basis to start a group. Steven was equally keen, keener still that he be the frontman. Edwyn, for now, acquiesced to guitar and backing vocals while taking charge of suckering whomever he could to fill their rhythm section.

Another school friend, a Clash plagiarist surnamed Duncan and thereby 'Dunx', was roped in on bass while local Fonz-a-like Geoff Taylor agreed to play drums after Edwyn dangled the false hope that one day they'd cover the Cambridge water torture of his favourites, Pink Floyd's 'Shine On You Crazy Diamond'.

Needing a name, James believed they should wear their musical hearts on their sleeves and call themselves The Punks. Steven and Edwyn were of the stronger opinion that not every spade need call itself a spade and turned instead to the name of James's guitar model. The Nu-Sonics.

Swizzed out of the Sex Pistols the previous Christmas, that May Saturday Glasgow's brave, wise and taut of trouser poured on to the regular Queen Street shuttles like evacuating refugees. Their destination was Edinburgh's Playhouse theatre where The Clash were headlining their White Riot tour above the school-uniform fury of The Jam, the fuzzy knee-trembles of Buzzcocks, the oppositional sneer of Subway Sect and the Amazonian brain haemorrhage of The Slits.

For The Nu-Sonics it was a baptism of English inner-city fire, catapulting them homewards pursued by the half-hollow threats of punk-loathing neds, dizzy with the din of the Westway barnacled to their ears. They'd arrived early in the day, hoping to express their punk allegiance by helping the bands carry in their equipment. They asked The Clash, whose drummer, Topper Headon, answered by throwing badges at their heads. They fared better with Manchester's Buzzcocks, a band they'd loved ever since a local tearaway called Frank brought their debut *Spiral Scratch* EP into the school common room, the ricochet of '*Boredom, bu-dum-bu-dum*' sending skyrockets of stimulation through Edwyn's young synapses. Original singer Howard Devoto, the one *Sounds* likened to the Boston Strangler, had since left, replaced up front by guitarist Pete Shelley, who invited the nascent Nu-Sonics to sit in on a fanzine interview conducted, to their horror, by a macho poser who kept making crass remarks about 'poofters'.

The summit with Shelley proved itself a double catalyst in the days that followed as the normality of school failed to restore order in their newly adjusted nervous systems. For

Edwyn, it flowered in the Gainsborough-shades of 'Blue Boy', a lyric he wrote to purge himself of the anger he felt towards the fanzine fool. For James, it wet the typewriter ribbon of their own rival publication, named by adding a fat 'No' to the logo of American entertainment magazine *Variety* and allowing him column space to air the raging humanitarian grievances he otherwise hid so skilfully behind his linen cheeks. Specifically his campaign against the Scottish football team's friendly in Chile, to be held in the very stadium where General Pinochet's military junta had imprisoned then murdered opponents to his dictatorship. With the ten copies of *No Variety*'s first issue photocopied by Edwyn's mother, his words were certain, he hoped, to make new Scotland manager Ally MacLeod's cufflinks tremble.

A fortnight after seeing The Clash, the *No Variety* editorial team were loose on home turf for a weekend double-header of New York noises. On Saturday night, the Ramones supported by Talking Heads at Strathclyde University. On Sunday night, Television supported by Blondie at the Apollo. This time there'd be no badges pelted at the Nu-Sonics' heads, only superior vocabularies flying above them. James asked Talking Heads' guitarist Jerry Harrison what he thought of the Sex Pistols. 'I think they're rather dogmatic,' said Harrison. James had no idea what that meant.

The second issue of *No Variety* increased its circulation to a mighty 25 copies but any chances of a third were quickly sapped by the energies now devoted to The Nu-Sonics. While Steven touted their existence to the editors of other fanzines, describing them as acolytes of Buzzcocks, Subway Sect and

New York punk, Edwyn and James twanged a repertoire of originals out of a flossy ether of inspiration and mimicry.

Their songbook now included James's 'London Weekend', an account of a pilgrimage down south to inhale the defiant aroma of Patti Smith via *On The Town* ('*Three little sailors dressed in white, drinking Coca-Cola and eating Marmite*'), the erratic changing tempos of 'Strawberry Switchblade', the virtual tinnitus called 'Time To Develop', some cymbal bangs and humbucker wallops known as 'A Good Cast', a sure-fire number one nowhere but the land of the daft entitled 'You Guys', Edwyn's 'Ready, Get Set, Go!' and a valiant translation of the title theme to *The Mary Tyler Moore Show*, 'Love Is All Around (You're Gonna Make It After All)', albeit for the most part valiantly unrecognisable. With these and other arrangements woolly enough to insulate a Hebridean crofter's loft, The Nu-Sonics braced themselves for their public debut in the bleak 'Mull Of Kintyre' winter of 1977.

Safely tucked over the Renfrewshire border seven miles away in neighbouring Paisley, the Silver Thread Hotel had fast established itself a blessed oasis beyond the jurisdiction of Glasgow's district council. The saviour who first entertained the brainwave of booking touring punk bands to play the Silver Thread's function room was the self-styled 'Disco Harry', a woman's man, no time to talk, whose own silvery threads implied he muttered 'The Hustle' on bended knee each evening before kissing a bedside altar to Travolta as he switched out the lights.

Disco Harry's ally over the iron curtain was an employee of the central Glasgow branch of Bruce's Records, Arthur

Haggerty. A pink-suited spiv in red-framed glasses who loved skanking to reggae and managed local punk band The Backstabbers, enterprising Arthur organised buses from Bruce's to and from the Silver Thread – immortalised ever after as 'The Punk Rock Hotel' – ensuring Disco Harry was never short of trade.

Some forty pairs of eyes witnessed the unveiling of The Nu-Sonics, who came, saw and spontaneously combusted over Disco Harry's floorboards. Like prisoners who'd made an escape pact only to waste their efforts burrowing separately in opposite directions they went nowhere slowly, laughing hysterically as their clumsy clods of noise buried them alive, witnessed by a gallery of slack jaws, wincing eyes and shaken wax unmoved by their plight.

They didn't have long to lick their wounds before their next public display of enthusiasm versus ineptitude. One month later, the Friday before Christmas, they were coaxed into cannon fodder support for Haggerty's Backstabbers who'd been chosen as the main turn at the seasonal party for the Queen's Cross adventure playground in the life-in-your-hands suburb of Maryhill.

Into this valley of death drifted the five Nu-Sonics, rosy of cheek and crisp of hem, ready to deliver the Mary Tyler Moore theme to the juvenile hobgoblins of local gang The Maryhill Fleet, whose shipmates eyed them up as a cat might a new scratching post; a quintet of blank canvases whose every pore ached for the incision of blade, the stamp of shoe or the flay of bike chain.

Edwyn and James locked their eyes on their guitars and started nervously thrashing, nervous of the thrashing that seemed imminent whenever either glanced upwards. A pit of rabid gargoyles, chewing, gurning, spitting, challenging, their fidgeting hands smacking pool cues into palms, some carouseling around the hall in shopping trolleys as their blood-lust screeches cancelled out The Nu-Sonics' amplified fumbles and the impotent threats of the all-too-few adults present.

A baggy-trousered midget monster followed the scent of the kill to the front of stage.

'Oi! Poofs!'

James cast a sly look to Edwyn, who looked to Steven, who looked back to James with pale-hearted fear.

'Aye! You, ya poofy cunts!'

The vultures were circling.

The midget vaulted on stage, snatching the microphone in his porky fingers.

'Play some fucking Sha-woddy-woddy!'

Another of Satan's orphans hobbled forward, hand in tonic-suit pocket fingering something none of them dared imagine, lips twisted into as wide a grin as the last of their sugar-rotted fangs dared allow.

'Sha-woody-woddy, ya bams!'

A small chorus formed.

'FUCKIN' SHA-WODDY-WODDY-WODDY!'

The immediate peril faced by The Nu-Sonics was that in their preparation for Maryhill they'd sadly neglected to learn anything from the repertoire of Showaddywaddy: the rainbow-wardrobed, chart-topping rock 'n' roll revivalists whose replicated tones were now all that stood in the way between them and the nearest hospital.

Frantic looks were exchanged for one long, lingering second in which all hopes of them ever reaching the age of 20 teetered on the gangplank. Screwing all their courage to the sticking place, Geoff started a shaky beat. Steven recognised its Woddy-Woddy rhythm and, with a deep, desperate breath, opened his mouth and sang.

'Standing on the corner in my new blue jeans ...'

Edwyn, James and Dunx cottoned on to his coattails and began busking furiously as Steven led them charging through Showaddywaddy's 'Hey Rock And Roll', each stuttering note a slow reverse from bodily danger.

The wild dogs howled.

'Sha-woddy-woddyyyyyyyyy!'

And The Nu-Sonics lived to see morning.

It was the less fortunate task of The Backstabbers to calm the Maryhill snake-pit still stirring for blood, a now impossible feat they hoped to achieve with their impersonation of Iggy And The Stooges and a set including such pearls as 'Mess In My Bed' and ten minutes of repetitive noise over which their singer, 'Rev Volting', gargled the name of their native estate, 'BLACKHILL!' The tense chins of guitarist 'Jimmy Loser' and bassist 'Colin Allcars' could only jut for so long before the waters of their ruin finally broke, doing so the moment Rev stripped to the waist, smashed a pint pot into his torso and proceeded to roll around the floor as if already being assaulted by demon hoards. Whereupon the Maryhill Fleet set sail and turned his mime into reality.

The Nu-Sonics had been standing watching in the wings, the relief that they hadn't been the ones set upon on stage lasting only moments before an oncoming cyclone of fists and steel sent them sprinting pell-mell towards the only dressing room. A hair's breadth from harm, Edwyn bolted the door in a breathless panic. He and his bandmates had made it.

'AAAAAAAAAAAAAAAAIYEEEE!'

But others hadn't. They stared at the bolted door, listening to the abattoir squeals of human origin honking from the other side. As each second passed, the cries of distress grew fainter until silenced by a dull pitter-patter of thuds, bangs, grunts and the occasional metallic jingle.

The door wobbled with the sudden force of toe-caps beyond. A voice ringing with hot spit grunted through the keyhole.

'Sha-woody-fuckin'-woddy!'

A lone cackle. And then it vanished.

In the half-hour eternity it took the police to arrive, none of them dared utter a word.

5.

Having mercifully spared the spines of The Nu-Sonics, fate's cruel ministers turned their lazy attentions to their long neglected pawn of destiny called Alan. Who, to their delight, was quivering in a dustbin in silent prayer, ears pricked to gauge whether the thunder of boots pursuing him had ebbed sufficiently far enough away for him to risk clambering out of his stinking priest hole and slithering home.

Such was the price to be paid in the same age of 'Sha-woddy-woddy' for walking the mean streets of Glasgow looking, as he knew, 'like a fat Buzzcock' wearing a combat jacket with 'The Clash' stencilled on the back; or a Ramones t-shirt; or a tie bearing the initials 'L.A.M.F.' after the Johnny Thunders & The Heartbreakers' album title acronym for 'Like A Mother-fucker', a tie he'd had specially adapted by the fair hands of his unsuspecting mother.

'What does L.A.M.F. mean, Alan?' she'd asked, needle threaded at the ready.

'Let's All Make Friends.'

Mrs Horne smiled. 'That's nice.' And on she sewed, never stopping to worry about the fact that, as far as she could tell, Alan had no friends.

He'd been there at the Edinburgh Playhouse when The Clash played in May 1977, similarly baptised, less by the headliners than the primitive howl of The Slits and the unrefined racket of Vic Godard's Subway Sect. Watching the unapologetically wild on stage barely able to deduce which way up to hold their instruments was a thrill beyond anything he'd previously experienced. So too was the crowd, his glasses misting over at the skinny of trouser, the severe of hair, the proud of button badge and the familiar tourist from the land of Bowie: so misted over he remained blind to the glow of the Bearsden teenagers under the same roof, missing each other's orbits completely.

It would take another catalyst to affect a collision course: one who was also present that night in Edinburgh, who spoke to neither, missing the last train to Glasgow and making his bed in a derelict building behind the castle.

Rifling through the racks of a new second-hand record shop called Lost Chord, Alan's jaw unhinged above the cover of *Time's Up*, a brand new Buzzcocks bootleg. He asked the hippy owners how they'd managed to find it.

'There's this guy who brings us bootlegs in,' they confided. 'He'll be here again on Thursday.'

Alan made sure he was also there on Thursday and finally bullseyed the friend to justify his mother's embroidery.

His name was Brian, a fellow university wastrel who'd turned himself into a one-man bootleg vinyl cartel. A stick-in-the-mud punk purist whom perverse Mother Nature had chosen to trap in the body of a debt collector, he was taller than Alan but with similarly thick hair, similar NHS glasses and a face to poop a thousand parties. A couple of nags feigning mutual sufferance of one another, both discovered they valued the price of true friendship as measured in the precious currency of continual piss-take; Alan forever Brian's 'pathetic idiot'; Brian forever Alan's 'such an old *bore*'.

By even stranger coincidence, Brian, like Alan, had also grown up in Saltcoats, attending a different school. Both their fathers worked at the local ICI chemical plant. And both knew of another of Saltcoats' punkish coves called Donald, a philosophy student who Alan had recently met on the train commuting to Glasgow.

On the downside, Brian was also part of a loose Ayrshire contingent of square-baiting extremists with an inexhaustible appetite for swastikas and De Sade which they happily advertised on the pages of their own fanzine, *Chicken Shit*. His shock-headed comrades included editor Hugh 'Bandy Waterhole' and Edinburgh music student 'Janice Fuck', whose hobbies included being ejected from pubs for wearing a dog collar. In harmony with their own delicate *noms de plume*, Brian's *Chicken Shit* brethren had chosen to christen him with the generously ironic 'Brian Superstar'.

Alan found this as funny as he found them disgusting, which was considerably.

In a pique of bedsit boredom, Joe Orton mischief, Mel Brooks' *The Producers* and Do-Do cough tablets, he coaxed Donald into helping him assemble his own *Chicken Shit* spoof.

A false, deceitful, malicious monstrosity breaking every taboo of acceptable taste that had a name, it was shock-punk for morons, and Alan had every faith there were enough morons out there with two Sid Vicious badges and half as many brain cells who'd take it seriously. Appealing to its target audience as best he could, he stuck a swastika on the cover with a smiling sun in the centre and called the fanzine *Swankers*.

The anonymous *Swankers* was left on prominent display in Lost Chord, mainly for the benefit of Brian Superstar. Flicking through and seeing a collage of his face superimposed on S.S. uniform in 'Sieg Heil!' pose, Brian guessed the culprit in an instant.

It didn't help that another copy had somehow made its way into the cackling clutches of his colleagues at Listen, one of the main city centre record shops where he'd started working, and shifting bootlegs, in the basement. Brian's favourite counter companion was a kid from Bearsden who shared his joy at playing loud, clamorous punk to wind up any long-hairs who strayed down the staircase. A handsome kid in tidy clothes, which Brian appreciated, and seemingly popular with schoolgirls such as wee Clare from Mosspark who'd flutter in on the pretext of buying a Buzzcocks badge as a lame excuse for a close-proximity swoon. A kid called Steven, whose belly laughs at *Swankers'* Brian Superstar pin-up marked the first crash of Hornal tide upon The Nu-Sonics' shores.

The Nu-Sonics themselves had, unbeknownst, already crashed upon Alan in the early weeks of January 1978. Once bitten but not a bit shy, their first gig after Maryhill paired them, yet again, with Rev Volting and his Backstabbers, this time below former local Southside punks Johnny & The Self-Abusers, now Simple Minds, and newly signed Birmingham reggae revolutionaries Steel Pulse.

All four were doomed to the Tuesday night altitude sickness of Satellite City, the former Clouds disco above Glasgow's Apollo. As the first into the firing lines, The Nu-Sonics bravely trudged forth with the experimental 'Artificial Love', featuring a guest poem by hairdresser chum 'Andy Shoes' quoting Chic's current top-ten hit 'Dance, Dance, Dance (Yowsah, Yowsah, Yowsah)'.

Alan had only come for the reggae disco, his latest obsession now that the woofing earthquakes of Joe Gibbs and Gregory Isaacs had eroded his appetite for punk. But he arrived in time to see Edwyn on stage in a blue velvet blazer, one arm in a plaster-cast, gurgling gaily through The Velvet Underground's 'We're Gonna Have A Real Good Time Together', a track from their *1969: Velvet Underground Live* double album. Which meant Alan wasn't the only person living in Glasgow who owned a copy. The chances of which, to him, were outrageous. Alan was intrigued, even if they were rubbish: when the reggae started, he forgot all about them.

Still clinging on to his university course by all but a bitten-fingernail of attendance, Alan had already blown much of his grant on dub singles, even though they sounded fuzzy and lame humming from his ill-equipped Dansette. He longed for a regular night where he could feel them flapping his trousers from the bungalow-sized bass speakers their creators intended. The occasional disco aside, there were no reggae clubs in Glasgow. And so, to the surprise of everyone including his inherently shiftless self, Alan started his own.

'Channel One' was launched in the spring of '78 to a threadbare first-night crowd of the few curious punks and fewer hippy stoners who could be bothered traipsing all the way to Cinders discotheque in Partick Cross. As his first experience, Alan found the art of DJ-ing idiotically simple and insufferably boring; starved of human conversation, playing one record after another, hypnotised by turntable tedium, hour after dismal hour.

Still determined to make a success of it, he sent details of Channel One to the music press, his name finally immortalised in print when *Sounds* took charitable pity. 'A well-dread gent named Alan Horne.'

His developing taste for scam whetted, he tried to boost door takings when his next night clashed with a gig by ex-Buzzcocks singer Howard Devoto's new band Magazine at Satellite City. Alan had time enough to attend both, leaving the Magazine show early after spreading a wildfire whisper that Devoto and the band were coming to Channel One for an after party. Dozens believed it, hotfooting it to Cinders. When Magazine never showed, some of them started crying.

By early summer his reggae night was in danger of making a profit, the financial dividends of which hadn't escaped the notice of local racketeers, who weren't slow in reminding Alan of their terms and conditions, the continued use of his legs, and the harmonious twain they expected to meet between former and latter. Seeking any excuse to end the intolerable isolation of another night alone in the DJ booth, and having long set his heart on spending the rest of his life in the biped fashion to which he'd grown accustomed, Alan scrunched his hopes for Channel One into a wastepaper ball and lobbed it into the nearest bin.

A bin much like the one he was hiding in now, his life and all its disappointments flashing before his eyes as he hunched in the festering gloom.

Hiding from the hiding of strangers whose purpose it was to stamp the sense out of whomsoever they chose for walking the right streets at the wrong time.

Hiding from the hiding which might be his last, and the shame that all he'd ever leave behind to remind the human race Alan Horne had ever existed is one week of infamy as a 'well-dread gent' and a copy of *Swankers.*

Hiding from the steady spit-spotting rhythm of raindrops upon the dustbin lid like tears of laughter streaking down the cheeks of fate's cruel ministers above.

6.

Edwyn, too busy trying to temper his giggles at performing with his arm in a cast and remembering the words of 'We're Gonna Have A Real Good Time Together', didn't notice the puckered sneer and raised eyebrow peeking over the spectacles of the chubby malingerer loitering with the reggae armband in the corner of Satellite City.

By disastrous past Nu-Sonics standards their third gig was a vast improvement, partly due to a strategic reshuffle after the battle of Maryhill. Geoff had gone, forcing Steven's hand in foregoing his short-lived frontman fantasies, retreating behind the drum kit. Always the obvious star, Edwyn was now left to blaze his irrepressible strangeness centre stage. With a 'stookie' and a blue velvet blazer, he wouldn't be ignored.

The cast on Edwyn's arm had been his own clumsy fault. Now left school, he'd enrolled at the Glasgow College of Building and Printing where he'd accidentally sliced himself with a Stanley knife. A careless and carefree student, most days he chose capers over course work, preferring to make pretend two-foot-long joints out of layout paper, setting them alight then wandering around the corridors pretending to be stoned, smoke detectors screeching in his wake. The regiment of graphic design appealed much less than his own pencil portraits of The Velvet Underground's Nico, *femme fatale* of his dreams, or bloodily smothering a baby doll in ketchup, or dragging his guitar and Vox amp into class so he could polish his Jonathan Richman pickings.

A salmon flapping in the dunes of the Sahara was less a fish out of water than Edwyn at college, or so it seemed to the keen pair of eyes which one day fixed upon him as he ascended the stairwell, dazzled by his lankiness, his fringe, his sensible patent shoes, his drainpipe jeans and the tangible aura of blazing strangeness.

The eyes belonged to as queer a sprite as ever slipped on a pair of trousers. A second-year student who'd returned by the skin of his tiny teeth after a harrowing first semester squandered in a nearby graveyard smoking bongs and drinking cider under the corruptive influence of the class magic-mushroom casualty.

By the summer term David McClymont had surrendered all hopes of college, returning to his Ayrshire home of Girvan just in time for him and three friends to be arrested in a case of mistaken identity for the brutal killing of a local café owner. Only when the finger of suspicion shifted elsewhere were the charges dropped. But by then his name was already local mud. The curtain-twitching curse of small-town gossip hung around David's neck like a noose, each furtive gallows-glance another yank on the rope heightening his desperation to flee Girvan once again.

With much begging and pleading to his college tutors in Glasgow, they cautiously accepted him back, now one puff on a lunchtime bong away from permanent expulsion. And so he behaved himself, and worked hard, and tried his best to act a responsible second-year, which meant being much too superior to fraternise with any first-year greenhorn. Apart from one so furiously exotic that at first sight of this lumbering long-legged dandy hauling a Vox amplifier his throat dried, his heart fluttered and his pupils followed its trail up the staircase as a plague rat would a pied-piper. In a flash he'd forgotten all hierarchical student norms and scuttled with haste beside him.

'Needing a hand with that?'

Edwyn didn't, but the charitable offer so bedevilled him that a few flights later he and David were both at the top of the stairs, two strangers politely treading around one another in talk of guitars, their tongues gathering pace in decreasing circles until the inevitable embrace of first-name introductions.

David wasn't the sort of person Edwyn would ever have imagined himself befriending. He had an inherently impish countenance, an unsettlingly pretty face and hair that fell in coquettish licks down over his collar. His trousers still flapped and a stale must of joss-sticks seemed to linger in the threads of his jumpers like dust between the cushions of an old settee. He failed, miserably, the acid test of Edwyn's musical inquisition, his sins redressed in borrowed tapes of The Velvet Underground, Subway Sect, Jonathan Richman and the shaky rehearsal demos of The Nu-Sonics. He professed to some experience on guitar, but when challenged by Edwyn to demonstrate his ability revealed that experience to begin and end with a hesitant scamper through 'Roundabout' by Yes.

Punk rock had very obviously passed David by. He was a prog-fan, a scrag-end hippy, a wrong which Edwyn thought still young and malleable enough to right. He would be his own private experiment.

'Project David'.

* * *

Alan had decided way before the encore that David Bowie was a hideous bore. A selfish, heart-breaking bore who'd conned Alan into buying a theatre box so he could sit like The Muppets' Statler and Waldorf, hissing in mute disgust, hideously drunk so as to numb the pain of what felt a lifetime's betrayal. A bore who'd bewitched everyone, but Alan, into ecstasies of applause. A bore who would never even hear Alan's hiccupping 'Bastard!' sobs, swallowed up like specks of plankton by the whale of fawning thunder. A bore and a bastard who was once the star illuminating Alan's universe, now a sucking black hole mocking every second Alan had ever spent worshipping the voice, the face, the body, the pristine godliness. If he could have had all those pennies he'd once saved in a jar in the foolish 15-year-old hope of seeing the *Diamond Dogs* tour, he'd have flung every one with as lethal precision as his teary-eyed alcohol-skewed aim would allow at the wiry doppelganger cavorting upon the Apollo stage. But he hadn't, so he couldn't, only groan in sick misery and steaming hatred, awaking the next morning with a head thumping all the harder in the bitter knowledge tonight he'd have to go and see the same thing all over again.

The second night he at least had the crutch of company, the long-suffering Brian Superstar with his new friend from the record shop. Alan took an immediate shine to Steven. He looked 'like a wee boy' who'd been dressed by his mother. But he knew a lot about music, made great efforts to be funny with his anecdotal 'antidotes' and, crucially, laughed every time Alan mocked Brian.

Batting their usual barbed sweet nothings back and forth, the three of them congregated in the Apollo foyer, Alan hoping last night's meltdown had been a silly error of drunken solitude. Tonight, in company, Bowie may yet reignite the flames of desire. So they stood, and talked, and bitched about the state of some of the fans until they were ready to go in and find their seats.

And then it happened.

Somewhere in the back of his head, Alan remembered the face. It was a gauche face attached to a proud neck, poking out of a checked shirt, above a couple of wiry legs in blue jeans.

'Hi, Edwyn,' said Steven.

It was a funny face. Not funny ugly or funny weird, but funny in an odd jack-in-the-box readiness that showed its springs even when the mouth was shut. Alan chose his moment to flip it open.

'That's a shit shirt.' He jutted his chin at Edwyn's checks. 'Who'd you think you are, John Boy Walton?'

The jack sprung.

'Shut your mouth, fat boy!'

Alan's heart flip-flopped. Edwyn blazed with wonder. The air between them crackled with silent static and Detroit strings. And then Alan remembered the face.

He'd last seen it sticking out of a blue velvet blazer on stage at Satellite City singing 'We're Gonna Have A Real Good Time Together'. It was a nice face. He wanted to know more about the blue velvet brain behind it.

'Hurgh! Hurgh!'

Edwyn started laughing.

Alan's deadpan pose crumbled as the corners of his mouth twitched tiny curls. A great, glorious perturbation in nature had occurred and, for once, fate's cruel ministers were helpless to prevent it. The colour of his world had altered, his universe split in two. His yesterdays, a forgotten song, for life had changed its tune.

'We're gonna have a real good time together...'

7.

As Scotland sobered up to the World Cup shambles of Ally's Tartan Army, as *Grease* seeped through Smurf beards and rivers of Babylon into every crevice of the UK singles charts, so Edwyn and Alan spent the summer of 1978 similarly seeping ever deeper into the bedrock of each other's affections.

An expert trader in the stock market of ridicule, Edwyn felt as if he'd struck gold. Alan, with his flouncy tics and cocky twitches, sometimes missing his r's like Elmer Fudd, offered him endless masterpieces of mimicry; Edwyn's 'Alan' like an unimpressed wasp who'd rather buzz a sarcastic 'well done' than waste its sting. It was a portrait in sound as severe as Scarfe, as precise as Rembrandt. Alan loved it.

In the meantime Alan had decided to let bygones be bygones, or more accurately swankers be swankers, and ask Brian to join him and Donald in a flat share. The designated den of chaste iniquity was on Huntly Gardens, just north of the university where Alan had only managed to cling to his course, and more importantly his grant, by blaming lack of attendance on a nervous breakdown: a successful ploy albeit involving mandatory visits to a psychiatrist which, as a fan of Woody Allen, he enjoyed much as he might a pleasantly diverting matinée at the pictures.

Brian moved in with his small warehouse of bootlegs, the scientific marvel of his video cassette recorder, his copy of Iggy And The Stooges' *Raw Power*, which he played most mornings, full blast, until Alan responded with the deft Detroit *touché* of Smokey Robinson & The Miracles, and his guitar and amplifier.

It was the sight of Brian's guitar, a Vox teardrop just like the one Brian Jones had played, which made Alan take temporary leave of his senses and accept the offer to start a band, believing, wrongly, that whatever transpired they would, at the very least, look good on stage.

Brian Superstar, obviously, would play guitar. Donald Rat, as he would become known, would play drums. 'Alan Wild', as Alan now styled himself, would try his best to sing since he couldn't be bothered learning any instrument; he once picked up a guitar but put it down when it hurt his fingers.

Which left only a vacancy for a bass player, a position duly filled by the abrupt return of the stuttering dog-collared musical legend of *Chicken Shit* infamy, Miss Janice Fuck.

Together, they called themselves Oscar Wild, barely worthy of a footnote in rock 'n' roll history had Edwyn not made it his first mission to scribble it there in as large and ludicrous marker pen strokes as was humanly possible. Banished from the flat by Alan whenever Oscar Wild rehearsed there, he would pretend to leave only to sneakily creep back and listen outside the door, aghast with delight at how unimaginably worse they were than his own Nu-Sonics. Edwyn's favourite was their blind Buzzcocks stab at The Troggs' 'I Can't Control Myself', making mental notes of Janice Fuck's clucking vocal harmonies so he could mimic them later – with such accuracy that were, by chance, she to have met an early grave its effect would have easily struck renewed terror into the surviving members of the Fuck family that their dear departed Janice's spirit still stalked the earth in vengeful agitation. Nor would he ever let Alan forget that Oscar Wild's concert career began and ended in a village hall in Troon, trembling before a local chapter of Hell's Angels which, by the time Edwyn got hold of the story and inflated it into the weather-balloon-sized farce he desired, ended in something approaching Altamont on the South Ayrshire coast.

With these and other conversational whoopee cushions – that Alan had written a song called 'Woah, Woah, Dustbin' and asked to be known by the nickname 'Bunny Cuddles' – Edwyn took to Alan like a dog to a Frisbee, his humour so pungent in its vividly descriptive dyes that soon even Alan had trouble remembering where the truth of Oscar Wild ended and the grotesque pantomime of Edwyn's charades began. Nor did he care. Whenever his spirits sank he could always rely on Edwyn to yank him back to pristine health by resuming *The Alan Wild Show*, his magnified-by-thousands megalomaniac doppelganger guaranteed to send the original rolling on the floor in squealing hysteria.

Equally exhilarating diversions from life's otherwise sad routine came courtesy of another frequent visitor to Huntly Gardens. He was a wayward soul from a good home in

Bishopbriggs, cursed by parents who so resisted life in the late twentieth century that they sent him to secondary school in short trousers. Concussed by the violent blows of adolescence, he awoke in an epiphany of nihilistic abandon. Life was absurd, and should be lived absurdly with little care for petty laws or personal safety. He was, he discovered, picture-gallery pretty, a Pre-Raphaelite cherub from the neck upwards, a beacon of boyish beauty shining through the chiaroscuro of divinely decadent Glasgow nightlife. At any given time, depending on whatever dye he'd splashed upon his hair, he could be Dorian Gray, Alain Delon, or the Artful Dodger, skipping wide-eyed along Sauchiehall Street in a top hat, whistling tunes of his beloved Buzzcocks on his latest secret errand from Beelzebub. He was a rogue, a ruffian, a larrikin, a scurvy knave, a Scaramouche, a naughty boy by name of Paul. And so Edwyn christened him 'Paul Naughty'.

Naughty but preposterously loyal, Paul would turn his eavesdropping on Edwyn's grievances over the state of his equipment into the surprise gift of amplifiers and cymbal stands. The less Alan knew the better, and he already knew too much after the night Paul accompanied him home, stopping by a rockery in the front lawn of a nearby house where he lifted up a giant stone with a bright-eyed 'pssst!' exposing the hidden booty of a recent jewel heist. Alan wasn't surprised the morning CID banged the door of Huntly Gardens so hard it jangled the strings of Brian's unplugged Vox teardrop. They were looking for Paul, but found only Alan and Edwyn, an overnight guest who'd been rudely awakened to face the Strathclyde Inquisition, as good as naked in underpants and a pink shirt.

Alas, poor Paul Naughty could only burn his wax so fast before the wick extinguished. The final flicker came when he stole a car to go and see Buzzcocks in Manchester. He drove most of the two hundred miles without a single flashing blue light behind him. Until just outside Manchester, he stopped for petrol, filled the tank, then hot-rodded away without paying.

He was in Barlinnie by Christmas.

* * *

As Edwyn and Dunx rolled around the floor, flailing punches at one another, crashing into furniture and pranging guitars, James and Steven's expectations for that evening's Nu-Sonics gig rapidly perished. Dunx had been on Edwyn's probation for several months, his commitment clearly waning. Incapable of voicing his will to resign, he'd now resorted to self-sabotage, slicing his fingers so he couldn't play bass, thereby enraging Edwyn into the orgy of fisticuffs now spinning at James's and Steven's feet. Adding insult to self-injury, he'd also shown up in white flares and a Bob Dylan *Desire* t-shirt.

The concert was another of Arthur Haggerty's schemes, a 'benefit' for a local crofter at Hardgate town hall on the north-most fringes of Glasgow and, to the astonishment of nobody, was to be Dunx's last stand with The Nu-Sonics. Alan came along expecting little but strangely tickled by their cover of Smokey's 'Tracks Of My Tears' and the romantic quickstep of Edwyn's latest, 'Simply Thrilled Honey'.

Since it was too far and too late for Alan to return to Huntly Gardens, he accepted Edwyn's offer to stay the night at his mum's in Bearsden.

The house was in darkness when they returned, Edwyn

leading Alan as quietly as he could up the stairs to his bedroom where he flicked on the light with a silent 'ta-dah!' revealing the full gothic horror of his secret lair.

The first thing Alan noticed was the Norman Bates shadows cast by Edwyn's stuffed-bird collection. Then the earthquake of his carpet, a crunch hazard of record sleeves, scraps of drawings, scalpel blades, paint tubes, glue pots, guitar picks and loose coins. Edwyn threw him a spare blanket.

'Make yourself at home. Hurgh! Hurgh!'

Alan fussed and flapped, scraping aside the debris until he'd managed to create as safe an Alan-shaped space on the floor as chaos allowed before swaddling himself in the blanket and lying down. Edwyn climbed into his bed and turned out the light.

Alan chuckled. 'Goodnight, Jim Bob.'

'Hurgh! Hurgh!'

And they slept like babes.

Morning brought a bigger shock to Alan's system when they went down for breakfast and were greeted by Edwyn's mother, Myra.

'Morning, Edwyn!'

She wasn't like any mum Alan had ever seen before. She seemed too young, too pretty. Too much like Wendy Craig from *Butterflies.*

'Hi, Mum, this is Alan,' smirked Edwyn. 'He's a homosexual Nazi.'

Myra stared at Alan, who now wanted to die.

'Oh,' she blinked, looking him up and down.

'Alan's at university,' Edwyn continued.

'Really?' smiled Myra. 'What are you studying?'

'Um,' Alan twisted his lips in a weak and confused leer, the best his muscles could muster by way of a return smile 'Nothing. I've just dropped out.'

Edwyn shepherded him to the breakfast table, still sniggering wickedly.

Myra spoke. 'Would Alan like to meet Mackintosh?'

Alan looked at Edwyn with eyes which pleaded some enlightenment as to who or what said Mackintosh was and whether he would benefit from their acquaintance.

'Yes, he would,' grinned Edwyn.

'Say hello to Alan, Mackintosh!'

Fat Mackintosh wriggled in Myra's hands with meowing ferocity, one paw in her fingers which she waved up and down inches from Alan's nose.

'Good boy, Mackintosh!'

Placing the cat back down, she turned to fix the boys some breakfast.

'Mum's favourite album is *After Bathing At Baxter's* by Jefferson Airplane,' snorted Edwyn, his every teasing syllable a calculated pipette drop in the beaker of Alan's brain, awaiting chemical reaction. He shook the solution some more.

'And she really likes The Velvet Underground's third album.'

It was all too much for Alan's head to bear, first thing in the morning in a strange house with a stiff neck after bedding on a floor of scalpel blades surrounded by taxidermy. Only when Myra finally excused herself, leaving 'you two with Mackintosh', could he fully relax, resuming the discussion they'd started the night before about the now uncertain future of The Nu-Sonics.

'So that's Dunx dumped,' sighed Alan. 'Well done, Eddie. What are you going to do about a bass player?'

'All taken care of,' said Edwyn.

'You wanting Janice Fuck's number?'

'Stupid. No, I've got someone in mind. You'll like him.'

'Allow me to be the judge of that.'

'*Allow me to be the judge*,' Edwyn wasped. 'You're such an old woman.'

'Is it Mackintosh?'

'Stop it.'

'Aw. *Come on, Mackintosh.*' Alan patted his knee. '*Nice puss. You wanna come and play with Uncle Eddie and The Nu-Sonics?*'

'That's another thing,' said Edwyn. 'I've gone off that name. I was telling the others. I've got a better one.'

'The Old Sonics?'

'Keep this up and I'll spank your bottom.'

'Oh, nice *bore*.'

Edwyn dealt him a floppy slap on the arm with a spluttering 'Hurgh!'

'So what is it, then?'

Edwyn paused for a sip from his glass, leaving Alan dangling with an expectant 'well?' etched on his forehead. The suspense tasted delicious.

'Come on?'

Edwyn put the tumbler down, licked his lips, then picked it up again as if about to motion a toast. There followed a pre-emptive 'hurgh!' at the back of his throat. And then he put Alan out of his misery.

'Orange Juice.'

8.

The three members of Orange Juice sat around the table of a café on Byres Road in Glasgow's West End, all eyes and those of their newly-appointed manager fixed on the little creature who'd been summoned to join them at this appointed hour on an unusually warm winter's day.

Steven stared at the little creature, then turned to Edwyn, then turned back to the little creature, who seemed to have exactly the same fringe.

James stared at Edwyn, then turned to the little creature, then turned back to Edwyn, whose lips said nothing but whose eyes seemed to shrug an open court admission of, 'Here's one I made earlier.'

Alan stared at the little creature, and only at the little creature, and spoke as if the little creature was some deaf specimen in the reptile house incapable of understanding the human voice.

'Oh, Edwyn! He's fan-*taaaas*-tic!'

The little creature blinked.

'Look at him!' And they all looked at him. 'It's classic. He's just like a wee girl!'

The little creature blinked again.

'He's *greeeat*! Oh, Edwyn! Where did you find him?'

Edwyn had already told Alan he'd found the little creature called David at college, a shapeless block of Girvan marble which he'd been sculpting, in secret, with records, tapes, tape measure, scissors and private bass lessons, chiselling for week after week at the skinniness of his trousers and the cut of his hair until his masterpiece was complete. He had strategically bashed every last atom of the bong-smoking, flare-flapping, 'Roundabout'-strumming David out of his system until what was left resembled his own obedient Wee Edwyn, a small but fully functional crepe-paper copy of its creator's ego.

David, in turn, had been an unlikely emotional anchor for Edwyn, rescuing him from the dead-end of graphic design and college pranks by recently finding both of them a job at Glasgow Parks Department.

Since all Edwyn liked drawing was birds, fish and portraits of Nico, the post of leaflet illustrator seemed the ideal vocation, even if his daily failure to produce an excuse to incorporate a scraperboard likeness of The Velvet Underground's ice maiden into one of his nature trails was a constant source of disappointment.

There were days of lazy perfection when Edwyn led parties of boggle-eyed school children through the park, pointing out the various breeds of duck – 'over there, the ubiquitous mallard' – and fielding their questions about the cut of his jeans.

'Sir, are you a punk?'

'Yes, children,' answered Edwyn. 'I'm nature punk.'

And there were days of romantic agony when David would patiently counsel Edwyn about his latest romantic infatuation. He'd become besotted with a female colleague who was already spoken for, recounting every detail of every meeting, every nuance of every conversation, every pivot of her jaw and every flutter of her eyelids until Edwyn was driven half-mad by her toxic flirtation and David even madder by his hopeless gibbering. She told Edwyn she couldn't leave her boyfriend and his heart buckled and broke with all the force of the Tay Bridge disaster. David did his best to help shovel up the pieces, unaware that the largest shards were already imbedding themselves in Edwyn's head in words and music about pleasure, pain and cities of tears.

As part of the grooming process to sneak him into the band, Edwyn had purposely briefed David on what he ought to expect of the others: James, a blithe spirit away with the bees; Steven, increasingly the dissatisfied voice of under-rehearsed discontent; and Alan, who in the flesh was only two degrees below the boiling point of hysteria Edwyn had been impersonating for weeks in a demented adenoidal screech.

'Just like a *wee girl*!'

And here was living proof. David smiled politely as Alan finished his inspection, skipping back to his seat having spent the past few minutes circling his head like a potter scrutinising a wet vase spinning on his wheel.

'So,' Steven began, clearing his throat, the QC at the bar. 'How long have you played bass?'

David's mouth started to twitch but it was Edwyn's voice which leapt in its way.

'I've taught him all our songs. So he can play whenever we need.'

'Well!' beamed Alan, sealing the deal with a single clap of his hands as if to slam Steven's fingers in the door of all further debate. 'That's settled, then. David, you're in the band.'

Edwyn let out an approvingly goofy laugh. David grinned back at him, their mission accomplished. James looked at them both, not entirely sure what had just taken place, but smiled anyway. And Steven's eyes burned X-rays through Alan, through David, through Edwyn, through the café wall, for a thousand worried yards into the infinite distance.

* * *

Somewhere in that infinite distance lay Edinburgh: 'Auld Reekie', where time marched to a less hobnailed rhythm, where softer accents were ground to cut glass not throats, where tourists mingled with indigenous toffs, where the rain washed rich rivers of history between its cobbles, and sunlight striped shadows in the flutes of Grecian columns. And where the council fathers had already shown themselves more tolerant of punk rock's trespassing tempo than their Glaswegian opposites the moment they allowed The Clash's White Riot tour to smash and grab the Playhouse in May 1977.

The city's first punk peacock to stir double-takes on the main drag of Princes Street was a boy called 'Fritz', Fraser to his mother, a former pupil of Firrhill High School, where four other young souls of a future force stewed in general indifference to education. Their names were Paul, Malcolm, Ronnie and Davy, between them forming various connections since primary school but never coalescing as one until after Firrhill High had wiped its hands of any responsibility for their actions.

To the outside world, Paul Haig was a striking young fellow with a face like a Siamese cat who never smiled. Punk rock had already tried to kill him once in August 1977 when the car carrying him to a Generation X gig in West Linton crashed into a field. Two months later he was poleaxed by the savage murder of two ex-Firrhill pupils, 17-year-old Helen Scott and her friend Christine Eadie. Paul's employment history only added to the disconcerting drizzle in his complexion, a slow slip into Dante's Inferno starting in Jeffrey's Audio House where the blue-rinsed manageress banned him from playing the Television records he'd ordered in specially; next missing out on his dream job at Glasgow art school due to wisdom-tooth surgery that left him incapable of speech the day of his interview; and hitting rock bottom in the archives department of the local health board where he was left alone, nine to five, to microfilm Victorian medical records – emerging into the daylight each evening plagued by the hundred-year-old images of spina bifida symptoms scorched upon his cat-like retinas. Never smiling.

It took a missionary's son with doe eyes and plump lips to change the forecast in Paul's face. Malawi-born Malcolm Ross had stayed on an extra year at Firrhill, taking a job as a lawyer's clerk, though he too may as well have been archiving negatives of nineteenth-century pigeon toes for all it excited him. Familiar faces across the playground, they finally spoke at a friend's seventeenth birthday party. Both were obsessed with Television's *Marquee Moon* and both wanted to start a band along the same lines. Paul was already murmuring melodies into a tape recorder in his bedroom, sometimes in an uncanny spoof of Lou Reed. Malcolm was only just learning guitar. Paul offered to teach him some chords and invited him to a practice in the attic of his best friend, Ronnie.

A former boyfriend of the doomed Helen Scott, Ron Torrance had been wrecking drums since his early teens and was now wrecking cassettes at the Brian Drumm hair salon where he'd been taken on as a trainee, sabotaging the bosses' in-store Rod Stewart tapes so he could play his own funky punk favourites.

Along with a meat-and-potatoes punk livewire from Bruntsfield called Gary McCormack, Paul, Malcolm and Ronnie started thrashing in the attic as 'Tequila Sunrise', an ugly duckling of a name which one day swanned into the only slightly less ugly 'TV Art'.

The cross-dressing clods of Edinburgh University's Pollock Halls of Residence were first to hear TV Art as background noise at a student drag party. Sticking to a script of faithful Velvet Underground covers and their one bashful original, 'Good Time Girl', they flinched their way through lipstick jeers from the pastily-powdered faces of oafs in pink nighties, deaf to the sweet irony of so much Art lost on an audience of TVs.

Jumping attics from Ronnie's to Malcolm's parents on Colinton Road, they wrote and rehearsed until the unspoken scent of something amiss grew too much to stomach. The guilty skunk was Gary, sturdy of bass but sloppy of washcloth, for whom TV Art had become too floral an environment for his thick plectrums and even thicker tattie-sweats.

Another of Firrhill's old school ties, cute and curly trainee quantity surveyor Davy Weddell, was roped in to freshen the air around their bass amp. The final cast assembled, the sound of TV Art duly became one of garret-incubated gloom, melodies bent and twisted by the aerials jutting from the Victorian rooftops around them, words wrenched from the ghostly static of Burke and Hare silently crackling between roof slates and weathercocks. Songs that read like slogans of pain: 'Torn Mentor', and the closer-than-home death rattle of 'The Thoughts Of Helen Scott's Last Boyfriend'. Songs that could only ever be written by one who'd spent too long trapped in a basement blowing the dust off sepia slides of spina bifida.

Theirs was a thorny blossom, but not the only to flower among the city's Jekylling byways in punk's initial monsoon.

While Paul Haig was pulling himself out of his car crash, Clermiston's Davy Henderson and Leith's Robert King were among those who made it to Pantiles Hotel in West Linton to see Generation X, both under the false impression that the advertised support, Johnny & The Self-Abusers, may be a pseudonym for the Sex Pistols rather than the mewling pupae of what became Simple Minds. Both teenagers took the night bus back to Edinburgh, riding in top-deck circles around the city until daybreak ushered them back to lives each was now determined to escape in song.

Davy formed The Dirty Reds, a pot-giggling punk shambles learning bar chords by ear from Kinks records spun at 16 rpm, fighting their way through Iggy and Lou covers, crawling out of their beds late afternoons to chew mushrooms watching Batfink do battle with Harold Hambone and Hugo A-Go-Go.

Robert became 'Bobby Charm', the first of many precocious guises fronting the Scars, whose 16-year-old drummer answered to 'Plastic Mac', whose tunes snagged on the nerves like butterfly stitches, who wrote songs called 'Slime' and 'Bedsit Boredom' and another cut from the secret droog-speak of *A Clockwork Orange*.

Where punk had divided Glasgow, in licensing subterfuge and knee-jerk ned thuggery, in Edinburgh it found unity in new covens of camaraderie. Hope hollered up Cockburn Street in ways it only whispered up Sauchiehall. In both the Scars and The Dirty Reds, TV Art shared the same bills at the Wig & Pen and the same barstools at the Tap O'Lauriston.

The Scars would become the first local act signed to Fast Product, a new record label run from a tenement flat behind Edinburgh art college which so far had only catered for Marxist student punk and the sombre robotic honks of Sheffield's Human League. First over the finish line, the Scars shook their peers with fresh tremors of optimism that they, too, could make the same leap from the sticky boards of the Wig & Pen to turntable immortality.

With such wild fancies floating around his head, TV Art's Malcolm stood with one stone deliberately trapped under his shoe, dragging it on the pavement like the nib of a pen, half-wondering whether he was wasting his time hanging around outside Clouds disco in the hope of early entry to see Siouxsie & The Banshees soundcheck.

A stranger's voice, more puzzled than hostile, asked what he was doing.

Malcolm looked up and saw a well-dressed boy with eyes like a hovering kestrel's who, before the evening was through, he would know as a drummer from Glasgow called Steven. They watched the gig together, discussing the groups they'd seen and the groups they played in, parting their ways with the exchange of phone numbers and a mutual commitment to meet again.

And so, one night in Tollcross, serendipity sang its banshee song. West met East, Glasgow met Edinburgh and the band forever to be known as Orange Juice first entangled with that not-to-be-known-much-longer-as TV Art, far over the horizon of that infinite distance.

9.

It was one of those cold, crisp bright December days where the miracle of the human respiratory system could be seen in the choo-choo-train wisps dancing from the lips of every soul on every street. Two such baby dragon puffs now blew from the mouths of Alan and Edwyn as they walked, mission-bound automatons, south-eastwards to the heart of the city.

Alan had risen early, his dreams sweetened by the previous evening when Steven had turned up at Huntly Gardens straight from the counter at Listen brandishing a new release in his hands and a knowing smile on his lips.

'Alan,' he beamed, 'you've gotta hear this!'

Moments later, the pelvic supernova of 'YMCA' by the Village People sent blissful shockwaves through the zips in Alan's cushions and the filaments of his cheeks, just as Steven had predicted.

Edwyn had spent another night at Hotel Huntly, awoken by the early claxon of '*Young man!*' before he and Alan began their leisurely trail, stopping for a café breakfast before carrying down Sauchiehall Street, veering Clydewards to the thin alleyway threaded against a strip of railway arches where poverty dazzled with its infinite riches.

In Alan's new circumstances as a government-funded university dropout, in lieu of ongoing psychiatric assessment, a mooch through Paddy's Market had become more daily vocation than idle habit.

Edwyn too, when his park sketching rota allowed, found few greater joys in life than hunting treasure among the rain-forest of junk piled on boxes and crates or pedestrian-tripping clumps that spread like an uncontrollable fungus.

The smell of Paddy's Market was that of something over-boiled, something which may once have been meat, something definitely more dead than alive, something which hung in the air whatever the weather in a thin, gristly vapour. Men and women with over-boiled faces sat, slumped, or proudly stood, beside their tiny patch of over-boiled knick-knacks, the material scrag-ends of over-boiled lives combining as one in this cloudy broth of recycled humanity sloshing its tide from one end of Shipbank Lane to the other. There was nothing that mankind and its machinery had ever made which could spoil the taste of such a broth. There was no vase so cracked, no toaster so plugless, no kettle so crusted with the lime of half a century's hard-water brewing, no shirt so buttonless, no suit so unloved, no felt hat so unwearably olive, no left shoe so alone without its right, no book so stained of page, no record so sleeveless and greasy, no album cover so vandalised by crayon, no dining fork so twisted, no spatula so melted, no saucepan so scorched, no object however small so begging to be otherwise consigned to the nearest skip which wouldn't have added something to the flavour of Paddy's Market.

With well accustomed eyes and fingers, Alan and Edwyn picked, fondled, stroked, flipped, sniffed and tunnelled their way from top to bottom, adventurer explorers in search of lost gold, their hearts accelerating at the sudden unearthing of an original Troggs single, a jukebox evacuation of Motown, a gatefold copy of *The Velvet Underground & Nico* with peelable banana, an American label plaid shirt, a tweed blazer or a 1950s cowboy annual. Such were the nuggets awaiting those willing to wade patiently through the over-boiled murk, where every visit was its own education.

Today's lessons were a musty old children's book with funny pictures of cats and nursery rhymes about their various capers. 'When one wee kitten's in the house, it's all as quiet as a mouse.'

'Hurgh! Hurgh! Hurgh!'

Edwyn had to have it.

Just as intriguing were a pile of postcards of romantic Scottish scenery, the images embossed with what looked like record grooves. Edwyn picked one up, turning it in the sunlight to see that he'd been right. It was both. A postcard record. Edwyn bought half a dozen.

The postcard records were so fragile that when they returned to Huntly Gardens, Edwyn only dared play a couple lest their shellac suddenly crack, their sentimental skirls of 'The Skye Boat Song' lost for ever.

He was just as taken with his new suede jacket, the subject of envious enquiry from the rest of Orange Juice when they next assembled for band practice. David had speedily settled in thanks to secret interim rehearsals with Edwyn and Steven who schooled him in the vital rhythmic co-dependence of bass and drums, all strategically planned without informing James who, as a consequence, was always struck how far and how fast they'd progressed with seemingly minimum effort.

The Nu-Sonics had always been a strange mutation of punk aspirations, an eccentric work-in-progress casting fuzzy feedback shadows whose edges blurred between the shifting shapes of Jonathan Richman, Johnny Ramone and Rhoda Morgenstern. But the sound of Orange Juice was now settling into its own distinct hue, a deep shade of newness coalescing in the streaks between Edwyn's primary colours of Richman, The Velvet Underground, Motown and the scintillating disco of Chic. A blazingly strange sound, which James further embellished with his odd country twangs, a fretboard Morse-code tapping from Memphis via Bearsden like the lonely telegram of a young man who'd fallen in love with *The Last Picture Show* and never recovered. They sounded like no other band in Glasgow. Like no other band on Earth.

The sonic hurly-burly of Orange Juice in all its square-pegged mystery prompted a simultaneous revolution in their wardrobes. It was as if the music they were playing had sparked a collective decision to isolate themselves as far as possible from the emerging cult of the poser-ned: the flicked-fringe, silky-trousered, Bryan Ferry-loving tribes now developing from their tonic-suited, 'Sha-woddy-woddy!'-screaming ned ancestors one link down Glasgow's social evolutionary chain.

James set his sartorial bar by his older brother's record collection, inspired by the plaid shirts of Moby Grape and The Byrds, shunning Paddy's jumble for the fresh hangers of hiking shops, the finished article offset with his favourite Barbour jacket or a carefully chosen flash of tweed.

Edwyn picked and chose at random – a sailor's shirt with tar flap here, a pair of jodhpurs there – similarly smitten with plaid and tweed and anything vaguely resembling what The Beach Boys were wearing on *Pet Sounds.* He hated the album – 'barber-shop schlock' – but loved the cover. Edwyn's main sartorial ambition, as he told James, was to give the impression of 'a member of the aristocracy down on his luck'. In a cream-coloured Edwardian hunting coat, he couldn't go wrong.

David looked and learned from his master, following Edwyn's footsteps through the woollen hillocks of Paddy's Market, emerging in an old pair of battered suede fur-lined boots, grey houndstooth trousers and matching scarf. Steven, who was never less than crisply clean in his appearance, found David's deportment especially baffling. 'David,' he would quiz, 'why do you dress like an old man?'

David would look to Edwyn, then to Alan, then to James rolling his eyes to plaid heaven, then back to Steven, then to his feet and shrug with a blushing laugh.

'I like dressing like this.'

Which he did. Not that it satisfied Steven. Not that very much about Orange Juice satisfied Steven. Where Edwyn and James heard wayward and dreamy, Steven heard way-out and sloppy. Where they played to the stars, Steven could only measure the impossible distance it would take to reach them. And where Alan, Edwyn, James and David now enjoyed the bright, young company waiting to entertain them at Glasgow School of Art, Steven heard only vulgar pretence and hollow posing and, by degrees, shirked away.

James was the only one who'd actually qualified for a place at the art school. Their lone ranger among the creative elite patrolling the halls of Charles Rennie Mackintosh, he'd been accepted for the first year of a town planning degree he'd never finish, sadly denying future generations the only hope of a plaid-paved civic Utopia where Steve Cropper Square intersects Jacy Farrow Avenue.

In need of cheap soup and rich gossip, most lunch times Alan would wander to the Victoria Café, the social heart of the art school, open to students and casual interlopers, where the vain and resplendent gathered in conspicuous segregation according to their different artistic disciplines. Alan and Edwyn's catchpenny clothes stirred scornful laughs from the puffy new romantic posers of the fashion school, but complemented the surrounding second-hand fixtures and fittings, plucked from an original site in Govanhill which had been due for demolition until rescued and reinstalled by the architecture students. The queen of the Vic was a big Irish woman called Mona, who specialised in assuring all patrons that the soup was vegetarian as she hauled the thigh bone of some poor slain unspecified beast from the same bubbling cauldron, and whose short-fuse hospitality blew at regular intervals in her cutlery-bending yell, 'Get outta ma café!'

The aloof fashion fops and their equilateral hair-dos aside, the art-school crowd and those who buzzed around its café and weekend discos were a sweet, oblivious antidote to the nice bores Alan had suffered at university. They were funny, nutty, fascinating and, to Steven's barely concealed annoyance, invariably '*greeeeeat!*'

The roll call of human specimens read as follows:

A candied darling who called himself 'Lucy Lastic'; who knew 'they' could never touch him for dragging up Sauchiehall Street as long as he didn't wear women's knickers; who knew no fear when it came to roaring 'fab doll!' at men the size of shipyards; who knew no shame when it came to recounting the gory details of his latest straight-corrupting conquest with his starter for ten, 'I've just been shafted!'; and whose ultimate destiny in certain surgical procedures was beyond all reasonable doubt.

Jill Bryson, a pretty polka-dot Alice looking as if she'd missed the bus for Wonderland and ended up in Glasgow by mistake, living on the Great Western Road with her boyfriend and the rampant 'Lucy' in a flat below a dentist's surgery which rattled daily to the sound of drilling enamel.

Peter McArthur, Jill's boyfriend, a photography student and Southside punk who'd first befriended Edwyn at Glasgow College of Building and Printing, and later bewitched Alan with his shared love of Fellini, Pasolini, *Cabaret* and his unused ticket stub for the Pistols' phantom Apollo show.

Drew McDowall, a performance poet from Paisley, and his young wife Rose from The Wee Scone Shop. When not surreptitiously handing out free pies to fellow punks under her boss's nose, Rose also played drums in Drew's band The Poems, once joined on stage by Edwyn and James for 'a musical recitation' of the hunting scene from *War And Peace*.

Gerry Hanley, Alan's usual lunchtime companion, who allowed him to join her café table of angry women in boiler suits, monkey boots and cropped hair, who shared a flat with the painter Adrian Wiszniewski and who herself, sometimes, could be coaxed on stage by Alan for a spot of performance art.

The tweedy man out of time called Malcolm Fisher, sufferer of untold allergies and pianist of unending jazz flourishes, who danced with his hands glued inside his raincoat pockets, whose flat, a chintz flock and floral eyesore like something from *101 Dalmatians*, he shared with his similarly allergic sister.

And a punk graphic designer called Robbie Kelly, whose brother had very briefly strummed chords for the mythical Oscar Wild, and whose girlfriend, Anne, was usually seen pushing a shopping trolley down the street with a doll sat up front like a genuine baby.

As far as Alan was concerned, his new art school associates' rapturous reception to Orange Juice was an exploding plastic inevitability. He wouldn't be disappointed.

Detonation date was Friday 20 April 1979, as James Callahan took forlorn stock of his final hours in Number 10 and as Art Garfunkel's 'Bright Eyes' bunny-hopped at number one somewhere above the shaking body of Michael Jackson, the wondering why of Sister Sledge and the recently deposed yet eternally resilient Gloria Gaynor. The 1980s were but one catastrophic landslide victory and a few spins of the glitterball away. The perfect time for Orange Juice, a name so wrong that it had to be right, to yodel their first Lifebuoy-scrubbed 'hello' to the universe.*

Wearing their Velvet hearts on their sleeve, they'd prepared a backdrop of Andy Warhol-style prints of sixties model Jean Shrimpton. When some roistering halfwit walked up to the stage and threw beer at Edwyn, he wasn't that surprised. Their every stitch and semi-quaver was a conscientious objection to the hairy chests of rock 'n' roll orthodoxy, an Alamo Edwyn fought in his new 'Davy Crockett' raccoon-fur hat screwed tight around his temples. Orange Juice had harnessed the power to annoy without even trying. Alan was sick with pride.

Steven had suggested their support band, telling the guitarist they should ring and speak to Edwyn first. Edwyn's first question was, 'Do you like Creedence Clearwater Revival?' Malcolm gave the right answer and TV Art got the gig.

Returning the favour, and bridging the East–West divide, TV Art arranged their own show the following night back home in Edinburgh at the Teviot Row university union, flipping the bill with Orange Juice supporting. Malcolm recorded both bands on a standard tape player, giving Edwyn a copy as a souvenir. The quality was rough but, listening back, everyone agreed their fidgety vigour showed promise. Everyone except Steven.

---

* The 'official' date of Orange Juice's first gig is usually given as 20 April 1979, their evening performance in Glasgow School of Art's main live entertainment venue, the Haldane Building. Prior to that, in March 1979 they'd played a less formal and low-key lunchtime show in the art school's Victoria Café.

His frustration now festered like a cancer, invasive and inoperable, waiting to burst the bubbles of all who strayed too close to his concertinaed frown. On a group outing to see The Pop Group, whose recent melodic wreckage 'She Is Beyond Good And Evil' had become a shared favourite, David saw the demoralised envy deep in Steven's eyes. In The Pop Group's shiny new equipment, from their shiny new major record deal, Steven saw the comparative Paddy's junk of Orange Juice and all that they lacked. Nearly every concert he attended prompted the same depression until his insecurity became an epidemic gloom, spilling over in waves of self-doubt rippling with silent unease through David, James and Edwyn.

Alan reasoned Steven's change of heart was down to his new job. He'd left the counter of Listen and the droll repartee of Brian Superstar for a better wage dishing out the dole behind a grille at the Maryhill branch of the DHSS.

It was either that, or the corrosive influence of his new pal, Jimmy Loser. Steven had started hanging out with The Backstabbers' guitarist much too regularly for Alan's liking. Edwyn was no lover of Mr Loser either. Jimmy thought Edwyn just a poofy Jonathan Richman impersonator. Edwyn thought Jimmy just another punky ned. During one tense verbal standoff, Jimmy goaded Edwyn with his blade. It forced Edwyn to reassess his opinion of Jimmy Loser. To that of just another punky ned with a knife.

Running out of scapegoats, Alan thought the root of the problem might be David. Steven had never really warmed to David ever since he joined. Alan's solution was to play fairy godmother, packing them off to the pictures together to see whether they'd bond over subtitles at the GFT. They both had a thoroughly miserable time.

The 'Steven situation', as it had become in the war cabinet of Alan's mind, only got worse. Band practices became ever strained as Steven tried lecturing them on the virtues of Marshall amplifiers and solid-bodied Les Pauls. The final straw was a nonsensical argument about David Bowie versus Patti Smith which raged for so long that neither Alan nor Steven could remember why or who had started it. Edwyn tried to intervene, but both sides seemed irreconcilable.

It was clear to Alan that everything he liked about Edwyn was everything Steven actively discouraged. 'For God's sake, Edwyn,' Steven heckled him, 'walk like a man!' It was just as clear to Steven that Alan was a corruptive menace whom Edwyn should stop seeing altogether.

There'd been times – like the night he and Alan were chased by neds walking home through the park, when Alan scarpered while he stood his ground and took the bloody blows – when Edwyn thought life may indeed be better if he stopped seeing Alan. But, fly-heeled coward though he'd been, Edwyn knew he and Alan had become mutual addicts, chronically dependent on each other's phosphorescent wit. They were more than friends. They were foils. Andy and Lou. Joe Buck and Rizzo. Max Bialystock and Leo Bloom. Sally Bowles and Brian. Harold and Maude. Jane Fonda and Michael Sarrazin bound in their own elimination dance which, in all probability, would most likely end with one, or both, blowing their brains or the other's out. But there was still too much fun to be had. Too much fun to stop having.

And so Steven walked away from Orange Juice. Away from Edwyn's heckle-beckoning shepherd cries and James's chivalrous guitar prangs, taking his place behind the drum kit of Jimmy Loser's new band.

The Fun 4 were the cross-eyed phoenix flapping from the fag-ashes of Rev Volting and The Backstabbers, but not so daft that they lacked ambition to immortalise their din in plastic. Jimmy and Steven took inspiration from the independent success of Fast Product, the Scars' label in Edinburgh, asking Fast's founder, Bob Last, for advice and manufacturing contacts. The combined funds of the Fun 4 just about covered the £827 (and 63 pence) required for studio recording, acetate mastering, metal plate mastering, artwork printing and vinyl pressing of all 2,034 copies of the first single on their own label.

They'd chosen the company name of NMC, as in *No Mean City*, the title of a 1930s novel about life as experienced on a knife edge in the slums of the Gorbals, meant to mirror the Fun 4's sound they'd describe as 'straight from the streets of Glasgow and all that entails'. Which, in the case of catalogue number NMC010, entailed songs about dying in a lift disaster, thalidomide victims and 'Singing In The Showers', the main A-side, which they dedicated to Nazi war-criminal hunter Simon Wiesenthal. Presuming, thereby, that Mr Wiesenthal's hot pursuit of the Josef Mengeles of this world through the South American jungle would gather Godspeed thanks to some fuzzy distress about 'the lovely surprise' awaiting the many million Jewish prisoners gassed in the showers of Himmler's death camps and the encouraging 'Deutschland Uber Alles' guitar break by their esteemed soloist, Mr J. Loser, Esq.

A disc of dreadful note, the Fun 4 single nevertheless unbottled Steven's entrepreneurial genie, which soon set about granting a vinyl wish to TV Art. Since Jimmy Loser vetoed any hope of them joining the one-horse stable of NMC, Steven created a separate label, Absolute Records, for their simultaneous debut single. They'd already been in the studio for a couple of demos worthy of release, latterly with Nobby Clark, producer, singer and one of pop's proverbial nearly-men who'd forsaken superstardom when he left the Bay City Rollers seconds before their tartan stomp went pandemic. Steven's only problem was their name. His generous offer to fund TV Art's single came with one caveat. They had to change it.

Malcolm asked Steven if he had any suggestions. He had, even if it wasn't his own invention but one James had coined as a song title during The Nu-Sonics.

'Strawberry Switchblade.'

Sharp-edged, yes, there was nothing so sweet and fruity about the music of TV Art, nor the colour of their clothes favouring demob blacks and kitchen-sink greys scavenged from charity shops and their fathers' wardrobes. Malcolm quite liked Strawberry Switchblade's psychedelic aura, its faint echo of a lost 1960s garage band that might have appeared on a *Nuggets* compilation. Paul wasn't nearly so keen. They would have to think of another.

Malcolm remembered one used by some friends of his at the art college for their own makeshift band, who knocked about a cover of 'Rescue Me' by Fontella Bass. They'd joked about how they were going to pick the most pretentious, arty-farty new-wave name possible, coming up trumps with the doomed hero of Franz Kafka's *The Trial*. Malcolm was polite enough to ring up their singer, Mike, and ask if they'd mind TV Art using it. Mike laughed, and gave his blessing. Paul, Davy and Ronnie approved. So did Steven, who thought it sounded a bit like Uxbridge student rockers Fischer-Z.

'Josef K.'*

The obvious choice for the debut single was their best song, 'Chance Meeting', even if the fumbling electric-piano version they'd recorded with Nobby the Roller sounded like an ice cream van trying to commit suicide. The B-side, 'Romance', was a thankfully more fibrous throb of detuned bass and square-bashing drums, as black and treacly as the sleeve, a group portrait taken in the industrial wastelands of Viewforth, which Paul had developed and printed himself.

Josef K's amateur vibrations needed mastering before they could be pressed up, necessitating Steven's trip to London's Portland Place Studios where 'Chance Meeting' would be transferred to disc by the master of mastering, George Peckham. As was custom, George asked Steven if he wanted to add any message into the run-out groove beside his own 'Porky Prime Cut' signature. Steven didn't have to think too long, adding a private joke. His cheeky salute to what might have been, indelibly stamped on all thousand copies

* TV Art had already agreed to find a new name when they were offered a last-minute support slot to Adam And The Ants at Clouds in Edinburgh on 20 July 1979. They chose 'Josef K' that afternoon so they could tell the venue, making their live debut as such later that evening.

of Absolute Records ABS1 for the few fans of Josef K who bothered to look for it.

'STRAWBERRY SWITCHBLADE.'

* * *

While Steven was scratching matrix mischief in London, back in Glasgow the very same words were sharpening in the minds of Alan and Edwyn as the title of a new fanzine. The combined editorial talents of *No Variety* and *Swankers* infamy were joined by James, David and their friend Peter, between them drafting an unstapled mess of ideas destined to remain an unstapled mess of ideas, from interviews with Bobby from the Scars and Viv from The Slits (who Alan loved talking to, only he couldn't be bothered transcribing the tape) to Alan's profile of Edinburgh ('a vast afghan coat disfiguring the landscape'), David's 'How To Have A Sex Change', and Peter's guide to shoplifting, with instructional tips from a light-fingered punk named Marge.

Strawberry Switchblade, Alan soon realised, was a waste of time and a potential waste of money after he was quoted a karmically-questionable print estimate from the presses at the local Friends of the Western Buddhist Order. Only by then, Edwyn had already persuaded him that it might make a good vehicle for Orange Juice, documenting their existence with a 'free' flexi-disc, picking a track from the bootleg Malcolm had taped at their Teviot Row gig in Edinburgh.

The chosen song was James's 'Felicity', as in happiness rather than *The Good Life*'s Barbara, not that he'd clarify the mystery. Edwyn once asked him to explain the opening line. 'What is the "it" they took away?' James answered 'concrete' and nobody was ever the wiser again. As one Italian analyst would later point out, it bashed a tune not unlike 'If I Had A Hammer' by Trini Lopez. But even through the rhubarb of Malcolm's murky audience recording, 'Felicity' popped like champers at Ascot and was therefore, by unanimous opinion, their merriest '*Woah! Woah!*' worthy of etching on to floppy vinyl.

Edwyn busied himself designing the flexi artwork, heeding the tattoo echoing from the pages of the musty old children's annual he'd picked up at Paddy's Market. It was his favourite illustration in the book: a trio of kittens gathered around a piano, one hitting the keys, one tooting on a trumpet and a third sat on the floor bashing a drum. It seemed apt and emblematic of the raw, cute and playful pawings of Orange Juice themselves.

The fanzine still a mess, the flexis yet to be pressed and paid for, Alan and Edwyn continued to talk, plot, dilly and dally without ever getting round to the actual doing.

On drab autumn days they'd sit in their favourite café, the long, narrow Equi, still clinging on to the 1960s at the far end of Sauchiehall Street, discussing only the things they didn't want to do.

On bored days they'd seek capers with their friends Peter and polka-dot Jill, visiting her parents' house down in Shawlands where the three boys decided to drag up. Peter looked like he'd failed an audition for *The Rocky Horror Show*, Edwyn strapped himself in a turquoise corset, padding his bony chest with satsumas for breasts, while Alan found that in wig and lurex smock he made a strangely attractive blonde. 'Look at me,' he giggled in the mirror. 'I'm beautiful.'

On mild days, they'd take daytrips into the country in the Austin Maxi Alan kept on semi-permanent loan from Major Horne. They'd root around mysterious, dilapidated manors or walk in woods and forests, where Edwyn loved playing pranks, pelting Alan with slimy brown pine cones, pretending it was his own faeces. 'I say, did I ever tell you about my perversion? I like to shit then throw it at my chums!'

But on no days would they ever 'go to the pub'. Drinking was strictly for neds, not sophisticated rakes such as they. Edwyn didn't drink; in all seriousness, he preferred orange juice. Alan, in his more abandoned moments of Alan Wild, only liked Babycham. He was a café flower, not a pub weed.

And so it was in a basement café on Queen Street over some greasy cheese and tomato toasties that the fate of the Orange Juice flexi-disc was finally decided. Alan and Edwyn chewed bread and fat while their fellow disillusioned *Switchblader* Peter sat watching Edwyn fussily fork floppy slices of tomato out from between his toast. Between them, they were trying to agree what to brand the flexi, much like a proper record label. Edwyn had many theories, but no names. Alan's best suggestion was 'Plastic Records'. They chewed on.

Peter listened to them brainstorm, his eyes wandering to the café counter decorated with postcards. It reminded him of the old playable postcards Edwyn had shown him.

'They're a bit like flexis,' Peter interrupted. 'Those postcard records you got from Paddy's.'

Alan slowly chewed his toastie. The precipice of 'Eureka!'

'Postcard records?'

'Yeah,' Peter nodded. 'Or you could call the flexi, "I Wish I Was A Postcard".'

Edwyn looked over at Alan. 'I Wish I Was A Postcard?'

Alan didn't say anything. Nothing good. Nothing bad. He just sat, and chewed, and thought. And secretly began to purr.

10.

By the time they received stock of all 2,500 copies of the 'I Wish I Was A Postcard' flexi, *Strawberry Switchblade* had been officially abandoned. Meaning, for the time being, 'Felicity', the bendable plastic debut by Orange Juice, was now a lonesome prize robbed of its intended raffle.

Orange Juice themselves had been persevering since Steven's exit with a new drummer, Chris, who'd briefly been a twig on the sorry sapling of a never-to-be-sketched rock family tree called Oscar Wild. Aesthetically, Chris wasn't right, a fashionable mod type who stuck out against Edwyn, James and David like Paul Weller trying to gatecrash Enid Blyton's Famous Five. Musically, Chris was even worse, racked by nerves, forever slowing down and frequently complaining as if drumming were some cruel form of hard labour. 'Edwyn,' he'd whimper, 'I cannae play. Ma wrists hurt.' In the past they'd been used to heckles of, 'You're all poofs! Apart from Steven.' Now, with Chris, they were merely all poofs.

The two-pronged problem, how to shift the 'Felicity' flexi and how to coax Steven back into drumming for Orange

Juice, thus tempering their perceived poofiness – an impossible task so long as they insisted on playing 'Lovesick', its thumping Motown doof-doof-doof drums a red rag to the bullish ned chant 'Poofs! Poofs! Poofs!' – called for the same solution. They would make a record. A proper one.

Steven had already shown how comparatively easy it was with the Fun 4 and Josef K. They could include the flexi as a free gift. Alan was equally confident that the scheme would be enough to tempt Steven back, if only as a moonlighting session drummer on loan from Jimmy Loser.

The money, an estimated £400 or so, they could also raise between them, with Alan the main shareholder borrowing from his dad. David would handle the sleeve design. Which left only the question of what to record and where to record it.

Of the few decent contenders, opinion was unanimous that the strongest was Edwyn's song which started life as the lovelorn 'I Resist' until further adornment, and a bassline shoplifted from Electric Light Orchestra's current chart hit 'Last Train To London', resulted in the self-deprecating disco of the sublime called 'Falling And Laughing'. His most successful experiment yet in trying to sound, simultaneously, like Chic and The Velvet Underground, it wasn't so much an unrequited *cri de cœur* as a life's mission statement; one which not only told the outside world as much as Edwyn ever dared about the true feelings of his blazingly strange soul, but shed as much light as could ever be shone through the prism of his see-sawing friendship with Alan. *'I want to take the pleasure with the pain.'*

For the B-side, they chose a chirpy instrumental written by James. Originally entitled 'Woodstock', with the accompanying hippy-dippy lyrics '*Let's go to Woodstock, baby, flowers in your hair...*', it was renamed 'Moscow', owing its new title to James's political interest in Russia's involvement in Afghanistan, and its hopscotching hookline to the roots reggae of 'Trod On' by Culture – details which had next to no bearing on the tune itself in all its apolitical, skankless joy.

The arrangements rehearsed, the sides decided, the final hurdle was the recording itself, an entirely alien process to both Alan and Edwyn. Using the little knowledge they'd gleaned from Steven – who mercifully agreed to help, and drum, as an act of charity for the strained friends he considered total incompetents – they booked the same studio where the Fun 4 had recently torn their emotional requiem for holocaust victims from the depths of their snotty nostrils: a tiny reel-to-reel bunker hidden at the back of a clothes shop in Strathaven.

A shortbread-tin-pretty market town 25 miles south of Glasgow, Strathaven, or 'Strayven' as local tongues insisted, was once home to Harry Lauder, the tartan music-hall minstrel with the jauntily perched tam-o'-shanter, knobbly walking stick and whisky-eyed twinkle, who dedicated his life to challenging the outside world's preconceptions of the indigenous Scotch peoples via such fierce stereotype-shatterers as 'That's The Reason Noo I Wear A Kilt'.

Nearly thirty years after Lauder died, his spirit still clung to Strathaven, its every bonnie nook and couthy cranny threatening to cough his kilted phantom skipping out of the nearest bush; slithering through cracks in the masonry; or from between the tweedy rails of John McLarty Tailors & Outfitters, the threshold of recording history upon which Orange Juice now stood shivering, less in excitement than in the Arctic suffrage of a snowy December day in South Lanarkshire.

Beyond the non-competitively priced mackintoshes and knitwear, through a curtain at the rear, lay the studio itself, such as it was: a cramped eight-track cubicle officially known as 'Emblem Sound', primarily used for radio jingles, the Lauder-esque squeaks and squawks of accordion bands, and the 'Christian psychedelia' of McLarty's own holy-rock label Emblem Records.

The good lord was certainly foremost in Alan's thoughts as he was ushered into the mixing pantry, feeling considerably less like Berry Gordy Jr. than he had five minutes earlier. He'd driven over with Malcolm from Josef K, a comparative studio veteran on hand to smooth out any lumps in their technical inexperience as best he could.

Edwyn and the rest of Orange Juice had arrived by bus, beginning their historic day of rock 'n' roll as they meant to continue by bounding on and off, swift as hares, without paying the driver. Their adrenaline pumping with the moral satisfaction of having felled no greater an oppressive Goliath than the Glasgow Omnibus Company, they set up their equipment while Alan outlined their musical objectives to Mr McLarty and the salivating dog sat beside him.

'The snare sound,' said Alan. 'We need it to be "Dancing In The Street". Kinda like that.'

'"Dancing In The Street"?' Mr McLarty repeated in a tone usually reserved for repeating some exotically named dish in defiance of translation on a foreign menu.

'Yeah,' said Alan, hope fading fast until finally extinguished when his eyes glimpsed the grim gimlets for sale on display in the shop out front. 'We're not going to get that, are we?'

Mr McLarty didn't hear Alan's pessimistic mumble, his full attention now diverted to the petting of his dog, administered with such relish that James ceased tuning his guitar transfixed, as he now was, by his new producer's physical intimacy with said flechy beast.

Against such sonic doubts and canine distractions, Orange Juice managed to commit their songs to tape as successfully as time, circumstances and naivety allowed.

'Falling And Laughing' required Malcolm's extra pair of hands strumming guitar during the intro while both 'Moscow' and its variant 'Moscow Olympics' mix (an opportunistic appeal for airplay the following summer with the Russian capital due to host the 1980 Olympics) offered just cause for Alan to supply some vocal shrieks.

The session over in a couple of hours, Orange Juice were finished in plenty of snowball-throwing, slush-trudging time to catch the bus back to Glasgow. Whereupon, the same driver who they'd cheated that morning held them to ransom with four full return fares, a 24-carat bollocking and a snivelling apology to the Glasgow Omnibus Company.

Nothing, however, could bring them crashing down from the euphoric heights of having cut their first record. Nothing, that is, until they sat with Alan and listened back to the tapes, the faces which had earlier been frozen by Strathaven chilblains now twice as rigid with the shock of sudden defeat.

'Moscow Olympics' and 'Moscow' were passable but 'Falling And Laughing' was all stumble and no joke. The star of Mr McLarty's mix was Steven's bass drum pedal, which he'd insisted on overdubbing live, a dull thunk like a neighbour's broom handle slapping the wall in agitated rhythm demanding Orange Juice turn their amps down. Somewhere beneath, like a trapped squirrel fighting its way out of a flip-top bin, was the imperial romance of Edwyn's pop masterpiece. The song deserved better. But they had no money left to rerecord it. For better or worse, dull thunk and all, it would have to do.*

And so that almost-white Christmas of 1979, the decade sang its farewell song. In the bang bang boogie of Wonder Mike and friends. In the off-the-wall groove of Michael Jackson. In the angelic dreams of Abba and the similarly high hopes winging their way in a parcel from Glasgow to the Production Express pressing plant in France. The first single by Orange Juice, and the first from the parent label they'd had to create for that purpose.

Where the 'Felicity' flexi had only wished it, 'Falling And Laughing' could realise it. Alan agreed the name was perfect,

---

* Memories differ on how happy Orange Juice were with the recording. James Kirk recalls his immediate disappointment listening back, particularly with the strange drum overdub. 'I don't know who was responsible. Maybe the studio owner's dog mixed it? Whoever did, they ought to be shot.' Edwyn, however, remembers being nothing less than delighted with it as his first record and offered no critique at the time. 'If it hadn't made me happy to listen to it,' says Edwyn, 'I wouldn't have released it.'

as was the logo: the single drumming kitten cropped from the fusty old annual they'd found at Paddy's Market. Its fat, furry head cocked to one side, one beater aloft in its right paw, another in its left, striking its own bang bang boogie for the world to sit up and take notice. Of Alan. Of Edwyn. Of their pleasure and their pain.

The first beautiful beat of 'Postcard Records'.

BOOM! BOOM! BOOM!

ACT II
THRIFTLESS AMBITION

1.

In the sinister hangover of 1 January 1980, as glass-agony eyes and cactus tongues flickered in sorry heads uncorked of all reason, as promises of a brave new world were broken with dawn's picket-line-grey 1970s skies, the name of Postcard Records was still nothing more than a white-hot figment of Alan and Edwyn's quicksilver minds.

Sixty days would pass before the business was officially registered in Edinburgh on the unlucky leap 29 February. Until then, it existed only in giddy conversation, in 963 pieces of vinyl still awaiting manufacture and delivery back from France, and in the few scraps of company paperwork kept in the sock drawer in the wardrobe of Alan's new flat.

The flat was two floors up in one of the many once-affluent Victorian terraces stretching westwards out of the city, like a root reaching to be nourished by the mouth of the Clyde. Over 70 years had passed since its gaslights rattled with hansom cabs and bone-corseted alarm at the discovery of a wealthy 82-year-old spinster bludgeoned to death in her own home, landing West Princes Street its grisly repute just within the boundary of Glasgow's historic 'Square Mile of Murder'. The road dividing the houses on each side was long and straight, sliced by over a dozen cross-streets. The impressive stone façades remained but their tenants were no longer the murderable rich, rather the student and Pakistani poor, bringing with them a visible bohemian scruffiness to the high ceilings and sash windows looking out on to a silent street all but empty of parked cars; disturbed only by the occasional slow-cruising kind, drawn by the prostitutes dawdling patiently on the corner.

David was the first to find the sanctuary of Flat 2/R, 185 West Princes Street, sharing it with a horn player and a hippy whose constant fog of pot, dense as the dunnest smoke of hell, inebriated all creatures, from human to dust-mite, who dared cross their threshold. When the hippy and the horn player eventually moved out, Alan very gratefully moved in. He'd been adrift for months since losing the lease on Huntly Gardens, forced into an uninhabitable cold-water midden within perilous lynching distance of the nightly manoeuvres of the Maryhill Fleet. The stark shell of 185 West Princes Street was comparative paradise.

With one remaining bedroom to fill, David asked around the art school for a suitable flatmate of similar temperament to himself and Alan.

Instead, he found Greta.

Alan's first impression of Greta was that she'd spent most of her life crawling under barbed-wire and hiding in ditches trying to avoid capture from the Nazis. She dressed like an Eastern European peasant, as Alan once observed, 'because she *is* an Eastern European peasant.' Hers was the permanent expression of somebody who'd seen life's worst but lacked the will to recount the gory details, the eyes a food-shortage-queue stare of all-knowing, all-sad mute observation. Such was the visage that Alan now had to face every day in the spacious kitchen where the three wayward strays communed, if rarely cooked.

The 1980s would struggle to make their mark upon the austere fixtures of 185 West Princes Street, furnished with ageless post-war scavengings of coarse fabric, dark wood and three Hilda Ogden flying ducks. In these clean and frugal surroundings, Orange Juice would rehearse while Alan listened, neighbours banged and Greta sat like an immobile ghost deaf to the joys of their gay guitar prangs. It was a flat fit for old maids, or possibly young nuns. There was definitely something nun-like about Greta, her fingers forever raw with the coat of bleach she scrubbed into kitchen and bathroom floors in ritualistic self-flagellation, her bedroom a stark white cell with a single bed, a light-up statue of the Virgin Mary and two records by Ivor Cutler. There was something decidedly Mother Superior about David too, joining Greta in her neurotic hygiene regime, ferreting around the living room with a carpet sweeper looking, as Alan would tell Edwyn, 'like Charles Hawtrey mowing the lawn.'

The tangible existence of Postcard Records became ever more so the moment Alan nervously tore open the first box of 'Falling And Laughing' after picking it up from the docks in east London where it had been freighted from France. Knocked gently with the knuckles it made the same hollow plastic boom as a Motown or Stax 45. Held up to the light its grooves glistened with the same oily sheen. And there, at the disc centre, a blue label with the drumming kitten. No longer a figment but an incontestable fact.

Alan's joy was brief. Upon his Dansette at 185, the dull thunk hiccupped through the A-side like an in-built scratch. In its fast, fizzy guitars – like hummingbirds hitting a bug zapper – and its tin-cans-and-string Byronic yearning for heart's satisfaction, 'Falling And Laughing' was still a work of art, but a slashed canvas. With each listen, Alan's heart sank further through his guts. It sank deeper still when he tried alternating it between plays of The Velvet Underground's 'Pale Blue Eyes', and the sensory reality of the tangible reality of the first Postcard record flushed him into the sewers of woe.

Edwyn tried hauling Alan up as best he could with his manic Alan Wild pantomimes and counterweight of blazing optimism. But even Edwyn's armour cracked when they made their first sales pitches to Bruce's and Listen, the main record shops in Glasgow soon to be annihilated when Richard Branson opened his Virgin Megastore there that summer. The buyer at Bruce's opened up the pink sleeve, pulling out the single along with the free 'Felicity' flexi and a plain postcard overprinted with the kitten mascot. Then played it, scrunching his face at the thunk of the drum. Out of what sounded like charity, he agreed to take 'a couple'.

It was the same story in Listen. Alan and Edwyn's worst suspicions were confirmed. Apart from their few weirdo friends up at the art school, nobody in Glasgow liked them, least of all wanted them to succeed. In concrete hiss and shadow yell, in mocking glance and freezing cold shoulder, in stranger's threat and scared sprint home, its dark streets still jeered them. The morning would come when the city was theirs but, for now, Glasgow was still the dead of night.

In the kitchen of 185 West Princes Street, Greta stood gawping at Alan, who sat beside the tailor's mannequin, a birthday present from Edwyn and David coming with its own uncannily Warholish wig, which he'd added as a permanent fixture, perhaps for want of more animated company than Greta herself. David sat at the kitchen table, pretending to doodle, stealing furtive glances at Edwyn who, like Alan, was flicking through the back pages of the music press. Page after classified page of record shops and mail order catalogues in Newcastle, Liverpool and London. The faint streaks of day glimmering fresh hope in their dimmed hearths.

The simple arithmetic was staring them in the face. They still had over 900 copies of 'Falling And Laughing'. They had a list of names and addresses in the back of the papers. And they had the use of Major Horne's Austin Maxi, the means to take their coals to Newcastle and beyond. Moving and grooving, gliding and striding, they would become dashing knights errant. Sir Alan Wild and Squire Edwyn, pledging allegiance to the drumming kitten on a sacred crusade to the record racks and rock hacks of the miserable nation.

Heads swimming with flighty purpose, hands swaying with boxes of singles, they charged down the stairs to load up Alan's car. David asked them how long they'd be away.

'Ach, a couple of days,' said Alan. 'Any longer we'll send you a postcard.'

Greta said nothing, remaining seated, her 'Guernica' eyes following Alan as he closed the front door behind him. One hour later, she still hadn't moved.

2.

Galloping through the February drizzle, Alan and Edwyn zigzagged south, picking off what defenceless northern record shops they could along the way, storming cash register barricades, charming Geordie, Scouser and Yorkshireman alike with their tongues more silvery than a Tunnock's wrapper.

By the time they reached London, a confetti trail of 'Falling And Laughing' lay scattered among the nation's shelves in their brazen, peachy-cheeked wake. The capital now towered before them like a great basilisk daring to be slain by their meagre artillery of pink sleeves and flexi-discs.

They aimed their first volley at the press, copying the addresses from the mastheads of their favourite magazines, bursting into receptions, running after anyone they recognised from their by-line photo in the *NME* on Carnaby Street, brandishing the single in the air like a regimental colour, bedazzling *Smash Hits* with Alan's smoke, Edwyn's mirrors and their chivalrous Scotch brogue.

'We're from Postcard Records and we're here to see your music editor,' Alan announced in the fragrant foyer of *Cosmopolitan.*

'Um,' ummed the keeper of the gates of glossy heaven. 'Do you have an appointment?'

'Appointment?' Alan blinked. 'No, no. We're from *Postcard* Records.'

'Um,' they ummed again. 'Postcard?'

'Postcard *Records*.'

The ums hit a hat-trick.

'Look, just tell them we're here. He'll know who we are.'

Which she did, though he didn't, but he still came down, returning to his desk whiplashed by spiel, confused as to why he was now clutching a smelly copy of 'Falling And Laughing' and its even odder accompanying press release about the 'hardened mucus' in the eyes of somebody called Alan Wild. 'The phone is his drug,' it warned, 'and the head of Postcard Records will be calling you.'

With ravishing strides, they next sprang a surprise attack on the fairy godmother of the musically hopeless – Radio 1 DJ John Peel – loitering outside the BBC where they ambushed him as he arrived for that night's broadcast.

'This is Orange Juice, from Glasgow,' said Alan, thrusting the single into Peel's hands. 'All those Manchester and Liverpool bands you play. It's all a nice bore.'

'Pardon?' blinked Peel.

Alan bristled. 'You need to wise up, old man. Forget all that Bunnymen and Teardrops shit. This,' Alan waved the single in his face for effect, 'is the future. Get wise to it now or you're going to look really stupid.'

That night the listeners of Radio 1 heard a perturbed John Peel tell them about the horrible, truculent youth from Scotland who'd harassed him on his way into work. As a precautionary measure to ward their evil omens from ever darkening his door again, just this once, he played 'Falling And Laughing'. And so the baby-steps of Orange Juice and the first dull thunk of the Postcard kitten beat out a victorious dot-dash upon the airwaves of the British Broadcasting Company.

Their arsenal all but depleted, the taste of triumph spurred them through their final skirmish with London's two biggest independent shops and mail order catalogues. Small Wonder in Walthamstow waved the white flag and took a hundred copies. Which left their last round with Rough Trade, the Notting Hill vinyl stronghold on Kensington Park Road attached to the independent record label and distribution warehouse out back.

The king of this castle was Geoffrey Travis, proverbially 'Geoff', a Cambridge graduate hippy in his late twenties who, as Alan immediately noticed, still had the gap-year-kibbutz look about the cut of his jeans and the kink in his curls. Alan's instant dislike accelerated once Geoff started talking to them without looking either directly in the eye, a detail which stoked fresh fires of animosity in Alan's soul. The inferno peaked when Geoff sat and listened to 'Falling And Laughing', all the while his lip pouting as its treble skirls vainly tried to penetrate the hessian cloth of his ears. He didn't like it but, recognising the tapping feet and bobbing heads of his co-workers, mercifully agreed to take two hundred copies with begrudging magnanimity.

Between their Travis inquisition and the last lugging of boxes from the boot of their Austin Maxi, Alan and Edwyn had time enough to browse through Rough Trade's racks at the competition and marvel at the surrounding walls, every spare inch covered with the staff's favourite record sleeves.

Among them was a rare Australian single Alan had heard Peel play over a year ago, loving it so much he cut out and kept its review in *Sounds* describing 'a clumsy tongue-in-cheek simplicity à la Jonathan Richman'. The band were The Go-Betweens from Brisbane and the song was 'Lee Remick', a gleeful tribute to the Hollywood actress of the same name who, as the lyrics noted, was '*in* The Omen *with Gregory Peck/She got killed – but what the heck?*'

While they were cooing over the sleeve – 'dedicated to John Fogerty, Phil Ochs, Michael Cole, Natalie Wood' – the girl behind the counter's ears pricked up. She was as surprised to hear these two starry-eyed Scots rave about The Go-Betweens as they were when she told them she knew the band. Her name was Judy, a fellow Queenslander, further startling them with the news The Go-Betweens were currently in London on an extended holiday, lodging in a hotel just up the road in Paddington.

All the while they'd been record-hustling, hippy-slagging and DJ-manhandling, the unresolved problems awaiting them back in Glasgow were never far from Alan's and Edwyn's minds. That, foremost, Orange Juice were still a band without a drummer, needing Steven back. And, second-most, Postcard was still a label with only one band without a drummer, needing Steven back: even if the blustering press release for 'Falling And Laughing' had alluded to non-existent forthcoming attractions by Drew's and Rose's band

The Poems and Alan's wild whim to inflict Greta upon the public as a half of a female vocal duo with their friend Gerry from the art school, 'The Shoo Lay Sisters'. Until this tantalising new ray of Australian sunlight.

Furnished with the address of The Go-Betweens' shabby hotel, Alan and Edwyn gallivanted their way to the front desk of the Welcome Inn, Sussex Gardens, and asked for their room number. They knocked and waited. There was nobody in.

With nothing to lose, Alan hastily scribbled an introductory letter, tucked it inside the polythene sleeve of a copy of 'Falling And Laughing' and shoved it under the door. The chances were they'd ignore it as the calling card of a couple of cranks. But at least they'd tried.

Several hundred copies of Postcard 80-1 lighter, the conquering heroes declared their crusade over and began their journey home in weary jubilance, growing increasingly weary and decreasingly jubilant as night fell in a curtain of rain and sleet.

Exhausted by their impulsive endeavours, their flagging spirits sank with every metre of the M1 hastening them back to Scotland, Alan hunched over the wheel, squinting through frantic wipers at the stormy blackness beyond like Janet Leigh in *Psycho*. Then the windscreen blew in.

They had no idea how. Whether gust, rock or the vile blows and buffets of fate's cruel ministers above. Alan pulled on to the hard shoulder to assess the damage. They hadn't any money left to find a garage and fit a new windscreen. Glasgow still lay another three hundred miles away. They had no choice but to soldier on.

The air blasted colder and the rain pelted fiercer. It felt like hang-gliding in an Arctic blizzard. When the rain turned to hail, Edwyn clambered to the back seat for shelter, mummifying himself in a blanket.

'Edwyn!' screeched Alan, blue hands fixedly hanging on the steering wheel. '*Edwyn!*'

A glum, chattering face poked up in the rear.

'I'm passing out,' Alan trembled. 'You've got to get back up here. Keep me awake. Just talk to me. Please!'

Edwyn gangled back to the passenger seat where soon his cheeks were the same bloodless bluish-grey as Alan's. When they finally reached West Princes Street, so withered and wild in their attire, they looked like two preliminary sketches of Munch's 'The Scream'.

A third, yet to move, was sat waiting to welcome them inside.

3.

The X-ray file named the patient as Nicolas Roeg. Robert Forster knew it had to be *the* Nic Roeg, film director of *Performance*, *Don't Look Now* and *The Man Who Fell To Earth*. Not that anybody would know from the orthopaedic radiograph inside. It could have been anyone's knee, only Robert knew, absolutely, it was the knee of a man who'd used it to crouch into a viewfinder looking at Mick Jagger romp on a bed with Anita Pallenberg, and Donald Sutherland with Julie Christie, and David Bowie with Candy Clark. And so, making sure that none of the nurses saw him, he slipped it inside his jacket. A sort of 'souvenir' of the time he'd spent temping in the records office of St Mary's Hospital in London. Something to frame and stick on the mantelpiece when he finally returned home to Brisbane, Australia.

Robert had been working at St Mary's only a few weeks, a last resort after the money he and his best friend Grant McLennan had saved to go travelling around Europe finally ran out. The trip was part holiday, part rock 'n' roll pilgrimage to the promised land they'd only read about in imported copies of the *NME*, hoping to turn around the fortunes of their own group which had recently run aground.

The Go-Betweens – Robert and Grant plus any drummer they could lay their hands on – had already released two singles in Australia, sending copies on an airmail wing and a prayer to the British music papers, John Peel and 'Roger McGuinn, c/o Los Angeles'. The promise of a deal with the UK branch of Beserkley Records, home of their beloved Jonathan Richman, collapsed when the label went bust. Having once been dangled the long-distance carrot of success overseas, Robert and Grant decided to grab it for themselves, leaving Australia for Europe in the autumn of 1979.

London was bitterly colder than they ever could have suspected, but sensually overwhelming. Stood on Oxford Street, Robert tried to grasp the enormity of their actually being there, feeling his brain couldn't cope, pouring his exhilaration out in a new song, 'I Need Two Heads'.

They fed their inspiration seeing as many bands as they could, three or four times a week, knocking in vain on the doors of major labels, who showed no interest in their arch and arty Australian pop. Nor did Rough Trade, Geoff refusing to release their second single, 'People Say', on the unfathomable grounds its Doorsy-organ sound was 'too commercial'. At least they had a friend in Judy behind the counter, who was kind enough to stick the sleeve of their debut 'Lee Remick' up on the shop wall.

The X-ray of Nic Roeg's knee pressed tightly to his chest, Robert turned the key in the door of the room he and Grant were sharing in the Welcome Inn and entered, a soft crinkle under his foot as he half-trod on something unexpected. He picked up the pink single with the words 'Orange Juice' on the front and a letter sticking out of the back. He read it and laughed, and was still laughing when Grant came back and they reread it together. The single intrigued them. The band on the cover didn't look like any they'd seen in London. They had floppy fringes, neck-scarves and a semi-acoustic guitar. One of them was actually smiling.

With no record player of their own, they waited until the weekend, when they visited some friends from Brisbane living across town in Highgate Village, a healthy trek up the hill from Archway tube on the Northern Line. There they sat listening in awe to 'Falling And Laughing'. It sounded exactly as they'd hoped the cover suggested. 'It sounds a bit like us,' laughed Robert.

They reread the letter again. An audacious invite to come to Scotland and make a record for a label called Postcard, who already warned them 'we have no money'. But after six months shivering in London having made no progress, it was the best offer any living soul had made them. Robert took a decisive puff on his joint, passing it to Grant with a stoned yet resolute twinkle in his eyes.

'Exactly how far away *is* Glasgow?'

* * *

Alan read it and laughed, and was still laughing when Edwyn called round to 185 and they reread it together. 'Thanks for your interest,' it began. 'We had to break into someone's house to hear the record. We found it interesting and a courageous effort, considering the musical climate. It reminded us of us!'

The Go-Betweens had taken the Postcard bait. Alan was determined to reel them in with the promise of Scottish gigs, the use of Orange Juice's equipment, and a willing drummer in Steven. He hurried off a reply that day. Over the course of another fortnight's correspondence, plans were put in place to accommodate the duo with their friends Robbie and Anne from the art school, making final arrangements to pick them up on Alan's next visit to London to see Subway Sect at the Music Machine in Camden.

This time it was Steven who accompanied him in the Austin Maxi, using the trip to mimic Alan and Edwyn's Postcard assault by trying to offload his Josef K and Fun 4 singles in Rough Trade. Still pinning his colours to Jimmy Loser and chums, Steven had recently splashed himself across two pages of Glasgow's *Evening Times* under the headline POP GO THE DIY BOYS, gaining local infamy as a 'social security clerk who thought he'd be a pop star'. The reviews in the national music press told their own story. The Fun 4's 'Singing In The Showers' provoked lukewarm Ramones comparisons while 'Falling And Laughing' made *Melody Maker* 'Single of the Week'. The social security clerk who thought he'd be a pop star would have to think again.

With his sheepish *au revoir* to Jimmy Loser and sheepier return to Orange Juice, Steven also surrendered all hopes for continuing Absolute Records, leaving Josef K looking for a home and Alan deliberating on whether to beckon them to Postcard.

His main reservation was their music. Josef K were in awe of the collapsing Mancunian star called Joy Division, hypnotised by the joyful joylessness of singer Ian Curtis and the blinding bright gloom of the music, looking for the means to conjure their own version of the same industrial northern black magic. Alan wasn't a fan.

Malcolm's love for Joy Division was devout enough for him to sell the electronic piano which had sabotaged Josef K's 'Chance Meeting' single so that he and Paul could afford the coach fare to watch them at the University of London Union in early February. They'd seen them once already, supporting Buzzcocks in Edinburgh, Curtis stealing the show with his voice from Valhalla and his flicker-book epileptic voodoo. Flogging their keyboard seemed a worthwhile sacrifice for a repeat performance. So they hoped.

The gig was dismal. Joy Division used it to preview new songs, each one a freezing gust from the crack of doom, which is precisely where Malcolm and Paul tripped and fell immediately afterwards. To save on accommodation costs they'd decided to brave it out till the next morning's return bus to Edinburgh on the benches of Victoria coach station. It didn't take long for Paul to snap, wandering off alone in search of sanctuary, finding an open apartment block where he tried curling under the feeble puff of a convector heater. A few sleepless, spine-cricking hours later he trembled back to Victoria, just in time to see Malcolm awoken by the groping hands of a loitering pervert.

Dawn dashed what sorry hopes they'd been clinging to through night's yawning peal of ice, insomnia and mild molestation. The bus they'd assumed would return them home that morning wasn't running. The next one was 10 p.m. that night.

Which, Alan reasoned when he heard about it, was what anyone deserved for being a sad Joy Division fan. Except his new conundrum was whether he wanted a band of sad Joy Division fans on Postcard. Alan pondered on.

The Subway Sect gig justified the journey: a joyous set of new Vic Godard songs with a pronounced northern soul influence, thumping in sweet unison to the Motown-tempos of Alan's musical heart. He'd brought his bulky boombox cassette recorder along to bootleg the show so he could share it with Edwyn, never expecting he'd be so enamoured with one song, 'Holiday Hymn', that Edwyn learned it straight from the tape so he could play it with Orange Juice. But though they scoured the Music Machine inside and out, there was no sign of The Go-Betweens.

Giving them the benefit of the doubt, Alan and Steven came back to the same venue the next evening. The Australians still weren't there.

Nor was there any sign of them in the Welcome Inn on Sussex Gardens. They asked Judy in Rough Trade if she knew where they were. She suggested the flat of their friends in Highgate.

When they called, a bemused Australian stood on the doorstep and scratched his head.

'Robert and Grant? They left two days ago.'

Alan felt the prize catch wriggle off his hook.

'Whadya mean?' he snapped. 'They were supposed to meet *us* in Camden two days ago.'

'Didn't say nothing about that, sorry,' shrugged the flatmate.

'So they're gone?'

'Yep.'

'Just like that?'

'Just like that.'

'Back to Brisbane?'

'Brisbane?' The Australian laughed. 'Nah, mate. They've gone and buggered off to Glasgow.'

Alan Horne. Still waiting.

THE POSTCARD RECORDS FAMILY

Above: Orange Juice. Left to right, James Kirk, Edwyn Collins, Steven Daly, David McClymont.

Left: The Go-Betweens. Robert Forster (top) and Grant McLennan.

Opposite top: Josef K. Left to right, David Weddell, Paul Haig, Malcolm Ross and Ron Torrance.

Opposite bottom: Aztec Camera. Left to right, Campbell Owens, Roddy Frame and original drummer David Mulholland in the kitchen of 185 West Princes Street.

THIS PAGE.

Top: Josef K's David, Paul and Malcolm take the Tardis to Planet Kafka.

Right: Boy wonder, Roddy Frame.

OPPOSITE: Edwyn and furry friends dead and alive, Sefton Park Palm House, Liverpool, April 1981

PREVIOUS PAGES: Daylight robbery. James, Steven, Edwyn and Alan, London, January 1981.

Alan again, naturally.

4.

Robert and Grant clambered off the train at Glasgow Central Station, one acoustic guitar and a suitcase each full of dirty clothes, shampoos and conditioners, a copy of 'Falling And Laughing' and an X-ray of Nic Roeg's knee, straight into the arms of the Postcard Records welcoming committee. Which consisted solely of David and his nervous grin.

They'd phoned ahead to 185 to say they were arriving by train, a message David had been unable to pass to Alan and Steven, currently hurtling back up the M1 in hot pursuit of their Australian pimpernels. Talking pop music and pleasantries, Robert and Grant walked with David along Sauchiehall Street all the way to the West End where, after dropping off their cases, they were taken to meet Edwyn, now sharing with two girls round the corner from 185 on Holyrood Quadrant. They entered to the rocking rodeo squeals of 'Almost Saturday Night' by John Fogerty, catching their first sight of Edwyn, crouched on his knees in front of his red children's plastic record player with a face of blazing intense scrutiny. He looked up at his visitors, casting his eyes up and down their frayed jeans, t-shirts and shaggy hair, arched an eyebrow and, foregoing all ceremonial how-do-you-dos, greeted them with the following:

'Do you think that second guitar is a Rickenbacker?'

The Go-Betweens' first summit at 185 came the next day when Alan returned, David sending him into immediate hysterics when he told him their Australian guests had long hair, reeked of pot and skinned up within half an hour of arriving.*

---

* Alan's 'official' version of events regarding The Go-Betweens' trip to Glasgow, as partly recalled in his own 1981 promotional *Postcard Brochure* booklet, is that of the Music Machine London mix-up, long hair and spliffs.

David McClymont remembers, slightly differently, that Alan was already there waiting for them in Glasgow: 'Before we knew it, a taxi was arriving outside 185 West Princes Street, with Robert and Grant inside. We had no idea what they were going to look like and, when the taxi door opened and Robert stepped out with long hair, Alan started running around screeching, "Oh my God, they're hippies, they're dirty hippies!"'

Robert Forster's own memory is as follows: 'The person who met us at the train station was David McClymont, and he'd been sent along, I only heard later, because Alan was scared that we were going to look like Elvis Costello and the Attractions. Like kicker boots and new-wave clothes. And, evidently, if we didn't look right we were supposed to be sent back on the train, or something. So it was just David, as a sort of scout, but we must have passed. As for being "hippies", that's another myth. Grant and I had shorter hair than anyone in Orange Juice. It's not as if we arrived in Glasgow with shoulder-length hair and suddenly got it cut. But this is Postcard so you're always shifting between myth and fact.'

Another such myth, claims Forster, is their alleged dope smoking: 'I can't remember it. Grant and I would have been as straight edged as Orange Juice. If we were getting drugs, the only people we knew in Glasgow were Alan and his friends, so how would we get it? If we were doing drugs, which we weren't, we could only get them through people he knew. You couldn't buy drugs on the streets of Glasgow. I wouldn't have known where to start. So, that's not true.'

'You mean they're hippies?' shrieked Alan. 'Dirty, stinking hippies? Oh, my god! Get rid of them!'

Sedated by a brisk walk to the near end of Sauchiehall Street, and a constitutional Equi knickerbocker glory, Alan's senses were cooled when he finally welcomed Robert and Grant, disarmed by their middle-class Queensland charm and their shared love of sixties Dylan and The Velvet Underground. He still couldn't forgive their smoking even if, secretly, Alan wasn't completely immune to the bliss of hashish himself. Their friend Jake, having been invited round for Sunday dinner, once plopped a generous lump into the pan of mince Alan was cooking. Once scoffed and digested it sent Alan into a euphoric if sloppy delirium, dancing like a rubber man around the flat to James Brown's 'Get Up Offa That Thing' until, having witnessed enough, Jake picked him up and threw him in the bath.

After their desperate winter in London, springtime in Glasgow was a blessed paradise for Robert and Grant, spending lazy afternoons in Kelvingrove Park, or on day trips to Loch Lomond, drinking tea in Equi, eating scones and toasting crumpets over the three-bar fire at allergic antiquarian pianist Malcolm Fisher's flat, or just lying around 185, casually helping themselves to whatever was in the fridge while Alan frowned on, dumbstruck by their gall, Greta brooding beside him in gulag-bound empathy.

Alan's only cause for distress, as far as they could tell, was Josef K, whom he'd finally decided to take on as a Postcard band. It was partly out of cynicism – sounding a bit like Joy Division meant they'd probably sell records – and partly out of a genuine hope that, with his and Edwyn's influence, they might brighten their colours. The clincher was when Alan heard Malcolm soundcheck, strumming the chords of Otis Redding's '(Sittin' On) The Dock Of The Bay'. Underneath all that brimstone Kafka and Camus gloom, the boy had soul.

Robert and Grant listened sympathetically as Alan paced up and down the kitchen like a general dictating manœuvres to his field secretary. Their ears still retuning to their host's accent, neither of them fully understood the nature of his complaint that Josef K were too 'doomeh'. There was nothing especially 'doomeh' about Malcolm when Alan took them to meet him in Edinburgh. Malcolm, primed for a day as unofficial tour guide to the city's Athenian architectural delights, was instead frogmarched by Alan back to his parents' house where The Go-Betweens made impromptu use of Josef K's rehearsal attic. Preoccupied as they were with strolls, scones and getting stoned, they still had urgent preparations for two gigs Alan had arranged to commemorate the tripling of the Postcard family.

Much to the stomach cramps of their leering Glasgow assassins, 'Falling And Laughing' had been an unexpectedly swift success, helped by a clutch of good reviews including the hallowed top 40-eyed pages of *Smash Hits*. Demand now dwarfed diminishing supply. They'd recouped enough to repress it, but 963 dull thunks were enough for one lifetime.

Instead, they would invest everything in recording three new singles, one by each band. Alan thought it was shrewd. Edwyn thought it was ambitious. Geoff at Rough Trade thought it was annoying.

'Oh, Alan,' he sighed down the receiver of 185. 'That's such a shame about "Falling And Laughing".'

'I know,' Alan humoured. 'But the next one's going to be miles better.'

'And you're sure you can't give us any more? Even if we press them?'

'We've made our minds up.'

'You have, Alan?'

'Yes, Geoff. We're expanding. We're going in to record Orange Juice, Josef K and The Go-Betweens next week.'

'Hmm. Well, I suppose...' The voice trembled like a cold compress to the forehead.

'Soon as they're done, I'll bring you down the tapes.'

'Oh, do that, Alan!' he suddenly raved. 'Do that. You must! I'm sure we can come to an arrangement over pressing and distribution. We'd love to have Postcard as part of Rough Trade.'

'Thanks, Uncle Geoff.'

'Sorry, Alan?'

'I said, thanks, Geoff.'

The keys to the kingdom now dangled before Alan's spectacles like a hypnotist's pocket-watch. What Geoff was proposing would transform Postcard into a national independent label. Rough Trade, in London, would cover all manufacturing costs and distribution for a percentage commission of profits while he, in Glasgow, would 'sign' the bands – not that Alan bothered with signatures, keeping the papers in his sock drawer to a bare minimum – book the studios and design the artwork without having to worry about any more epic quests in an Austin Maxi; choosing, instead, to run his empire sat in his regular back booth of Equi café, scratching inflammatory graffiti and scraping the last lick of cream from the glass of his knickerbocker glory.

Under James's banner FUNKY GLASGOW NOW, the three Postcard kittens – Orange Juice, Josef K and 'all the way from Brisbane, Australia' The Go-Betweens – were packaged as one and thrown to the lions, such as they were, of Edinburgh's Nite Club in early April. The Go-Betweens, with Steven on drums, wore warm, woolly clothes to match their warm, woolly songs, greeted by approving yelps from the few willing to believe their international notoriety suggested on the poster as a matter of fact.

Local luminaries Josef K went on last, their tunes midnight black and murder serious, ticking and whirring like clockwork panic. Sandwiched between, Orange Juice were a circus unto themselves, Edwyn the giggling ringmaster in his raccoon-fur topper, trilling '*Step we gaily, on we go!*' while James's guitar foxtrotted around David and Steven's rhythmic fandango.

Their obnoxious beatitude successfully rattled the cage of Alan's Edinburgh opposite, Bob Last of Fast Product. After their set, he scribbled them a note and sent it backstage: 'Go and join the Cockney Rejects and get killed!'

Not that it bothered Alan, otherwise engaged with singer Billy MacKenzie of The Associates and his intriguing offer to make a flexi-disc for Postcard covering the 'crumbliest, flakiest chocolate' jingle from the Cadbury's Flake advert.

The following week it was Orange Juice's turn to headline when the same bill played Glasgow Technical College. The gig was blessed by the unexpected good omen of a bad penny who turned up during the afternoon soundcheck, flapping through the doors, removing his top hat with a ceremonial flutter as Alan and Edwyn's jaws swung open in unison. The spritely glint in his eye was only a little dulled by things unspeakable at Her Majesty's pleasure. The young marquis of mischief, Paul Naughty, was free.

That night, Josef K defied all 'doomeh' expectations in lurid made-to-measure psychedelic shirts, visually more kaftan than Kafka, if not quite enough to upstage their hometown hosts.

'It's really *amaaazing* to be here tonight,' twinkled Edwyn. 'I hope you're all going to dance or pogo or whatever you do.' Which hardly anyone did, too transfixed to shake a limb while they watched and wondered which pigeonhole they could stuff this indescribable newness of gentrified country and western disco.

Orange Juice's impact was all the more inscrutable with the addition of guest saxophone player Gordon 'Gordy' McEwan, on loan from Edinburgh band The Cubs, squawking jazzy traffic jams through the dizzying 'Upwards And Onwards'. None watched prouder than Paul Naughty, now guest of honour at an impromptu prison-release party courtesy of Postcard Records, which part of him proudly hoped had benefited in some way from his stolen spoils of yore.

Both gigs ensured hopes were high when they finally went in to record the three singles in the last week of April at Castle Sound, a recently converted Victorian primary school in Pencaitland, a village east of Edinburgh. Believing only a mad Scotsman would be mad enough to come to Scotland and produce bands almost nobody had heard of, Alan had succeeded in luring ex-pat Glaswegian loon Alex Fergusson, former guitarist with Alternative TV, whom he'd sweet-talked during his and Steven's recent trip to London, tracking Fergusson to his YMCA lodgings.

The Go-Betweens were first in to record Robert's new London song, 'I Need Two Heads' – its tune betraying a susceptibility to 'doomeh' shadows of Joy Division in its ho-humming bass, if not in its frisky handclaps and peculiar lyrics about bank books and child detectives – and another they'd been sitting on since before they left Brisbane called 'Stop Before You Say It'. The morning of the second day at Castle Sound was devoted to Edwyn's 'Little Ladies' (as he sometimes called Orange Juice),* with Josef K cramming in what extra time they could that afternoon.

Alan and Edwyn had pinned their hopes on 'Blue Boy', the old Nu-Sonics favourite dedicated to Pete Shelley which, after two years of kneading and proving, had lost its clumsy stutter, maturing into a portcullis-buckling pop-punk fizzbomb. Fergusson captured its unsophisticated bliss, a fine romance between Burns guitar and Fender Champ amp, Edwyn whipping its '*curse*' and '*bless*' from a Dylan Thomas poem, James soaring off on a psycho-country guitar solo with added booster rockets from the 'Telstar' drones of a Vox organ borrowed from a wee ginger kid from East Kilbride. For the B-side they chose the bullish red rag to

* 'Little Ladies' after the fictional female band in the popular seventies TV series *Rock Follies*.

'Poofs!'-hecklers everywhere, 'Lovesick', its biscuit-tin Motown wallop delivered with similarly breathless vivacity.

With the few hours remaining, Josef K only had time to record one side. After the merrymaking of 'Blue Boy', their 'Radio Drill Time' felt like the harsh, sobering hangover, the sound of stainless-steel surfaces being swept in the aftermath of an industrial accident which took its lyrical cues from the sleeve notes of Lou Reed's sense-shredding noise experiment, *Metal Machine Music*.

Having made a record, and thus fulfilled the original purpose of their trip, it was time for The Go-Betweens to bid a fond farewell to Glasgow. Not before beguiling a local radio interviewer with tales of their supposed past-lives playing Sex Pistols covers on the Australian rodeo circuit, and taking their place in a group Postcard family photo session on the steps of 185 West Princes Street. Robert's enduring memory of Alan would be watching him wait just before the camera clicked to frame his face through a tambourine, like Andy Warhol on the inside sleeve of *The Velvet Underground & Nico*.

Going their separate ways, Grant went off for further adventures in New York while Robert returned to Australia. The spoils of his European travels amounted to James's original Nu-Sonic guitar on permanent loan, a copy of 'Falling And Laughing' and one slightly-creased X-ray of Nicolas Roeg's knee. And, most precious of all, Alan's promise to release 'I Need Two Heads' on Postcard once he'd sorted the deal with Rough Trade.

Alan was only a little sad to see them go, more relieved to preserve the chastity of his fridge and rid the air of their smoke. He stood waving them off on the kerb, then walked back up to his kitchen. To the domestic abnormality of 185 West Princes Street. To David and his carpet sweeper. To Greta and her strange habit of frothing her mouth with toothpaste and screaming out of the window to scare children for a laugh. And to the scrap of paper in Grant's handwriting left waiting on the worktop.

'Bye, Alan. Make us rich and famous.'

5.

The first car swerved clear. The second would have hit him if Edwyn hadn't dragged Alan's flailing body out of its path and back on to the pavement. Until now, Edwyn thought he'd gauged the full Richter scale of Alan's mental earthquakes, but this was a whole new Armageddon from which he feared his friend would never recover. He'd been staggering headlong into London traffic, looking a man only seconds away from spontaneous combustion who in the meantime was happy to risk the alternative ending to his sorry days squished under the tyres of a family saloon.

'Alan!' Edwyn pleaded, a firm hand tugging on his shoulder. 'You're going to get killed!'

'Good!' he howled. 'Fucking kill me!'

Alan tried to wrench himself off the kerb but Edwyn's grasp was too tight. He stopped struggling.

'Kill me!' he repeated, this time more a sob than a scream, his eyes filling up as he watched a lorry rush past and imagined his body ripped apart under its axels. And then he wept, cursing out his tears. 'The cunt!'

Edwyn offered an affectionate pat on the back.

'The stinking, fucking hippy cunt!'

'It'll be OK,' Edwyn patted.

'It won't be OK!' Spit popped between Alan's lips with every syllable. 'How can it be OK? That hippy fucking cunt! How can it be OK? He's fucking betrayed me!'

So Alan continued raging as Edwyn ushered him in stops and starts to the nearest available café, praying that a hot cup of tea may not only restore a drop of Alan's will to live but also possibly calm the demon who'd latterly taken such foul liberties with his mouth.

They sat opposite one another, between them two steaming cups and a polythene bag of reel-to-reel tapes which Alan had been clutching under his arm during his rush-hour Russian roulette with the deliberate intention of he and they being flattened together in a coarse mosaic of flesh, ferric and metal. They contained the new recordings of 'Blue Boy' by Orange Juice, 'Radio Drill Time' by Josef K and 'I Need Two Heads' by The Go-Betweens, fresh from their private audience with Uncle Geoff at Rough Trade who, after pulling a variety of faces the likes of which brought to mind nothing less gruesome than the slow-motion cudgelling of a freshwater trout, expressed such great disappointment as to withdraw his offer of a distribution deal – thus detonating Alan's current Hiroshima of reason.

'You know why this is, don't you?' he seethed. 'It's cos of "Falling And Laughing". He wanted us to repress it, and I wouldn't. He's trying to punish us.'

'We've still got the tapes,' Edwyn encouraged. 'We can take them to Virgin, try some of the majors.'

'You don't think I'm fit to run a label, do you?' Alan threw his arms over the bag. 'If you want to buy them off me, good! Gimme twenty-five grand and you can take them wherever.'

'You're mental!'

'*Me* mental? We've got no money left. We've spent it all on this.' He swatted the bag. 'Fucking tapes. They're useless. We might as well leave them here.'

Edwyn could only hope it was the speed talking. 'Alan?'

'Edwyn!' It was the cry of utter defeat. 'I'm drowning! I'm going under! I'm condemned by a society that demands success when all I can offer is failure! It's the fucking end. You don't realise? The fucking end of Postcard!'

* * *

They were 'doomeh' days in West Princes Street that summer. Sandwiched between the combative glooms of Alan and Greta, David decided to move out. He found cheerier chocolate-brown lodgings with two office girls and a cheerier-named upstairs neighbour Derek Diddums, hoping said Diddums would prove a more receptive audience to his own modest repertoire of songs including 'Bake The Cake' and 'Woman In A Man's Body' – neither of which were considered rehearsal-worthy by his fellow members of Orange Juice.

Even David's efforts to help Greta had gone awry. Sensing her financial embarrassment – unable to afford a normal packet of cigarettes, he noticed she'd instead pop to Mr Singh's corner shop to buy individual 'singles' – he offered to buy one of her paintings for £100. Greta agreed on condition she kept the canvas in her room so she could keep tinkering with the painting as she wished. The day David left, he asked Greta for a parting glimpse of his investment. She showed him. The entire picture was now coated in an even shade of black.

David's vacancy was taken by Brian Superstar, whose temperament did little to improve the domestic austerity. Shortly after moving in he awoke one morning to find himself in the middle of a bombsite. The ceiling had collapsed during the night, showering his bed in dust and rubble. He shook the clods of plaster out of his hair, stood up, brushed himself down and walked into the kitchen where Greta was stood motionless in the corner, as if the room were an elevator straight to the ninth circle of hell and she the infernal bell hop.

'Come here,' said Brian, and Greta followed.

'See this,' he continued, pointing to the collapsed ruins upon his bed. 'If you clear that up, I'll give you a fiver.'

Greta collected the dustpan and brush while Brian began counting his loose change.

Brian's arrival should have meant fresh sport for Alan, too irresistible a bull's-eye for his own acid ridicule, or cackling with delight at Edwyn's equally merciless 'Brian Buzzard' spoof, mimicking Brian's disparaging drawl and mechanical chain-smoking to a tee, or winding him up by deliberately picking up his pristinely preserved punk records with sticky fingers. But the suffocation of his current despair left no gasp for laughter. Joy Divison's Ian Curtis had just hanged himself and Alan seemed next for the noose, his face a human transistor for the nation's current number one, 'Suicide Is Painless'. Depression led to drink, and drink to depression, and the sorry cocktail of the two to pitiful nights of crying on shoulders and being helped home babbling incoherent agonies about hippies and betrayals.

The tether ran out the night Alan sat with his prized box of singles on his lap, the vital organs of Tamla Motown, Stax, Kama Sutra and Stateside scoured from Paddy's and thrift-shops, pulling titles out at random, reading out the labels in a cold, android voice like wind whistling through a kazoo.

'Lee Dorsey. "Operation Heartache".'

Then snapping them.

Greta just sat and stared. David and Edwyn begged him to stop. Alan kept delving and destroying. Then he threw the box on the carpet and joined it there, a sickly calf felled by the swift lasso of all-consuming grief.

Edwyn was worried. David was worried. Even Steven was worried. James would have been worried too had he not previously absconded on a camping holiday without telling anyone where he was going, or when he was returning; for all his bandmates knew he was a soggy plaid-clad corpse at the bottom of the Clyde.

The moon was down in Glasgow. Alan was down. Orange Juice were a man down. Brian Superstar's ceiling was down and Greta was Greta. So the isobars of gloom maintained their long rainy season inside 185 West Princes Street, impervious to the soft, summer breezes wanly wafting at the window panes.

* * *

Three weeks passed, wallowing in dismay until, fortified by chicken suppers, knickerbocker glories and the appetising thought of one day serving sweet revenge upon Uncle Geoff, Alan slowly recovered his wits.

He'd been determined not to return to his parents asking for another loan, but the volte-face of Rough Trade had left him no choice. The kitten was drowning. Postcard's only means of survival was to press the next single themselves, just as they'd done with 'Falling And Laughing', and prepare for another door-to-door sales crusade in the Austin Maxi.

Major Horne's generous investment was enough to inspire a cunningly economical plan to release two of the proposed three singles: Orange Juice's 'Blue Boy' and Josef K's 'Radio Drill Time'. They would save on costs by producing one reversible black and white sleeve which could be used for either, each band given its own share to hand-colour their side in felt-tip pen, scribbling, signing and defacing as they desired, subconsciously revealing the nature of the music within. Josef K, taut and controlled, meticulously shaded in their cover of the band's shoes around a potted plant. Orange Juice, carefree and gay, wreaked chimpanzee havoc over their Lichtenstein-style pop art design.*

---

* Orange Juice's share of the reversible 'Blue Boy' sleeves formed the basis of a 'colouring-in party' around the kitchen table of 185. As well as the band, various friends were roped in to help, including Peter McArthur, his girlfriend Jill Bryson, Drew and Rose McDowall, and Robert 'Hodgey' Hodgens. 'We started off trying to colour things in properly but it took forever,' says Jill. 'Eventually someone came up with the bright idea of grabbing all the pens together in one hand and then just scribbling round and round in circles, so that's what we did.'

Peter McArthur also recalls their wasted efforts to fly-poster adverts for 'Blue Boy'. The posters were all individually screen-printed by Peter, Alan and Edwyn at the Glasgow Print Studios, using as much free ink and paper as they thought they could steal without being noticed. The next night they took 'a circular route around the West End' pasting up their handmade creations. They returned to West Princes Street several hours

With these exquisitely vandalised wares, bold knights errant Sir Alan Wild and Squire Edwyn once more saddled up their steeds for another adventure down south. To save wasting money on the same old scabby hotels around Paddington, they took up the offer to stay with Harry Papadopoulos, a Greco-Glaswegian ex-maths teacher who'd ditched his set squares to photograph maniacs in bands for *Sounds*, now living in a house in Willesden with a young theatre manager and fellow Glasgow ex-pat called Grace. Charmed to within an inch of her life, especially by Edwyn, Grace took an immediate shine to the pair, as much impressed by their dandy wit as their iron will to walk the five miles on foot to the centre of town, laden with boxes of singles and endless reserves of bluster. Alan and Edwyn, in turn, found Grace such an agreeable host that thereafter they commandeered her house on Hanover Road as Postcard's regular London home from home.

The tremors of their previous 'Falling And Laughing' trip hadn't been forgotten among the record shops and music papers they revisited with a comforting sense of déjà vu. All were pleasantly stunned by the dramatic leap forward of 'Blue Boy' – even the BBC's once-bitten 'nice bore' John Peel, who was prepared to forgive his shuddering first impressions of Alan and play it at least twice – while behind the inky clatters of the once school-bullied wretches of the London weeklies,

---

later. 'The doorbell rang,' says Peter. 'Alan went to see who it was, and called Edwyn and me to see. Someone had followed us, torn each limited-edition handmade poster down after we'd pasted it, collected them up and, whether as a joke or out of spite, re-posted them all crumpled and torn over the landing walls of 185.'

a raptor in need of fresh meat now began considering 'the Postcard phenomenon' as ripe for their talons.

The raptor was Irish, name of McCullough, who funnelled his passions into hot metal for *Sounds*: a fanatical scribe with an eye for blooms not yet tainted by the adjectives of any fellow fickle trendsetter, whom he alone could champion with a to-the-grave betrothal. Until he found the next one.

Postcard Records was such a bloom, one which inevitably lured McCullough on a fact-finding mission to Glasgow and into the bosom of number 185. His two-page report, ostensibly on Orange Juice and Josef K, was instead dominated by Alan, who effortlessly hogged his Dictaphone and its column-inch offspring with his diverse opinions on Factory Records and Edinburgh rival Bob Last's Fast Product.

'Pathetic.'

Where McCullough and *Sounds* led, the *NME* followed, sending their dangerously clever northern overcoat called Morley a month later. Alan found Morley another 'nice bore', pumping him with propaganda that he and Edwyn were 'going for the charts' and that Postcard were 'the only punk independent because we're the only ones doing it who are young'.

Morley found Alan 'a morose kid in transparent spectacles', a description reinforced by the unflattering portrait in the accompanying spread. The photo, taken by their old *Strawberry Switchblade* ally Peter, bore an unsettling likeness to the sour mush of Throbbing Gristle singer Genesis P. Orridge, if not the kind of Central Station bag lady reeking of

Vat 69 who dupes suckers with the old 'left ma purse on the train' routine. Peter printed up a copy for Edwyn as a joke, not anticipating Edwyn would find it so hilariously ugly he'd send it straight on to the *NME* picture desk.

'Dear *NME*,' wrote Edwyn on the back in his best fake-Horne-hand. 'If you're planning any "Postcard" feature for forthcoming issues, please use this official "MR POSTCARD" pic. Love, Alan.'

They used it. 'Mr Postcard' exploded, but the apocalypse was brief. Sands were shifting, tides were turning and winds once insufferably ill now rattled the letterbox of 185 in hopeful whispers. The words 'Postcard', 'Orange Juice', 'Josef K' and 'Alan Horne' were smudging the pages of the London music press too regularly to be ignored. Vindication was only a phone call away. Alan had already written the script and learned his lines. The day it rang, he was ready for his close-up.

Brrrrrrring! Brrrrrrring!

All silence on set at 185. Cue Alan. And – 'Action!'

Mr Postcard lifted the receiver from its cradle with an impatient, 'Yes?'

'Alan?'

He recognised Uncle Geoff straight away. He pretended not to.

'Who's this?'

'It's Geoff.'

'Geoff?' Mock surprise. 'I wasn't expecting you to ring, Geoff.'

'I know, Alan, but I have some great news.'

'Oh?'

'Yes, Alan. You know, I've been listening again to "Blue Boy", Alan. It's such a gorgeous record. Really, it is.'

'You think so?'

'Oh, yes! It's lovely. Really lovely.'

'Hmmm.'

'So we must have that chat about Rough Trade and Postcard.'

'What chat's that, Geoff?'

'As we were saying.'

'Saying?'

'About distribution.'

'Remind me, again?'

'From now on with Postcard, we'll pay for everything and we split it fifty–fifty.'

'Fifty–fifty?'

'Same as we do with Factory.'

Alan pulled the receiver away from his mouth, wheezing like Muttley.

'Alan?'

Decorum restored. 'Fifty–fifty? No, I'm not gonna do that, Geoff.'

A pause. 'I thought you might say that, Alan.'

'Uh-huh?'

'I did, Alan. And you know what, Alan?'

'What, Geoff?'

'Just for you, Alan, because I love these records so much, I'm going to make Postcard a special deal.'

'Special?'

'Yes, Alan. I'm prepared to go eighty–twenty.'

Alan's heart skipped. Fireworks. Champagne. Life is a cabaret, old chum.

'Eighty–twenty?'

'Rough Trade pay for everything and we split it eighty to you, twenty to us.'

'I'll have to think about that, Geoff.'

'Do think about it, Alan. Come down, soon as you can, soon as you decide, and we'll sort the paperwork.'

'OK. I'll let you know.'

'Bye, Al—'

Click. *Brrrrrrrrr!*

Two days later, Alan was sat in Rough Trade's new offices in Blenheim Crescent. He saved the last throw of the dice until they were face to face, at the precise moment Uncle Geoff poked a pen towards him, ready to sign.

'Eighty-five–fifteen,' smiled Alan. 'And then we've got a deal.'

The contracts had already been drawn up. 'All income arriving from sales of the above mentioned record (less 20 per cent distribution charge) will be given to Postcard.'

The pen hovered in Geoff's fingers, like a relay baton in freeze-frame.

Alan stared at it, saying nothing, moistening his lips.

The baton drew back. Geoff turned the contract around so it faced him, smiling feebly, struck through the number '20' and initialled '15' in the margin.*

He twisted it back around to Alan. The baton, again.

'And I want accounting every three months.'

The baton drooped.

'Three months?'

'Three months,' smiled Mr Postcard. 'You can add it in that wee space at the bottom there.'

The wee space at the bottom was filled and the baton passed. Then, with a slow deliberate flourish of the aforesigned 'A. C. Horne', the victorious kitten banged its drum.

The relay was won.

---

* Geoff Travis's conflicting account of his negotiations with Alan and Rough Trade's terms with Postcard is as follows: 'We offered to take them on. It wasn't a ludicrous deal in the way that Alan Horne said it was, where they were going to rip Rough Trade off and change the rules of the record industry because I was so desperate to be involved with them. That's not true. I think that sounds like nonsense. But for me it was just exciting. I hold my hand up and say I didn't hear, the first time I listened to "Falling And Laughing", that it was a work of complete genius, but sometimes it's hard to do that. But I did soon come to recognise that they were doing something really, really good.'

Copies of Rough Trade's original contracts for several Postcard singles were passed on to this author by Alan. They confirm the terms were, as he claims, an exceptional arrangement of just 15 per cent distribution charge, the remaining 85 per cent to Postcard (less the manufacturing costs).

6.

Sleep was deep and dreams were sweet in 185 West Princes Street. Alan dreamt he was a cuddly tabby cat, twitching his whiskers and bashing a drum on his bedroom floor. His wardrobe burst open with a landslide of vinyl until he was up to his furry ankles in sleeveless singles and albums. Each one bore no information other than the Postcard insignia and kitten mascot. He picked one up at random and placed it on his Dansette with eager paws. It was the gentle throbbing beat of 'Pale Blue Eyes' by The Velvet Underground. Alan purred in satisfaction.

From somewhere under the rippling spillage of records a telephone rang. He rummaged around until he felt the receiver and held it to his soft, downy ear.

'Alan?' It was Geoff.

'My name's Catman,' hissed Alan. 'I make purrrfect records.'

'I know,' soothed Geoff. 'That's why I'm sending you a new contract. One hundred per cent to Postcard.'

'Purrrfect!'

He meowed with delight as shiny gold coins began raining from the heavens, bouncing off the drum, the floor, the turntable and the bed where Lou Reed lay topless under the covers, raising a knickerbocker glory in his hands with an inviting cheers. 'We make purrrfect records, Alan.'

Prrr!

'Alan.'

PRRR!

'Alan?'

He opened his eyes and found himself in his usual back booth of Equi café, surrounded by graffiti, looking directly at Edwyn over a steaming hot Ribena. A slightly confused Edwyn.

'You were purring,' Edwyn told him.

'I was what?'

'I was talking to you and you were away with the fairies.'

'You must've been boring me.'

'And you were purring.'

'So,' Alan blushed only slightly, trying to shake the pristine image of a semi-naked Lou from his head. 'You were saying?'

As Edwyn was saying, now they'd won the deal with Rough Trade their tongues had much more urgent matters to trumpet.

Edwyn had already designed a new standard single sleeve which could be used on all future Postcard releases, copying a bucking cowboy on a Wild West landscape from an old Roy Rogers annual he'd found in Paddy's. Alan added the lettering, frustrated with the wonkiness of his Letraset skills until Edwyn assured him it didn't matter: as an antidote to the slick sleeves of Factory, the askew art of Postcard was a strangely charming asset.

Most important of all, Uncle Geoff's money now meant they could finally put out The Go-Betweens' long-delayed

'I Need Two Heads' as well as two brand new Orange Juice and Josef K singles, released head-to-head.

Orange Juice's 'Simply Thrilled Honey' was another of Edwyn's old Nu-Sonics tunes, a sarcastic rebuff to promiscuous female advances from his own high romantic balcony. Its galloping melody teased with false promise of a heroic crescendo, but even with its Johnsonian '*Ye Gods!*' chorus, whirligig finale and additional synthesizer hoopla from Malcolm, it never hit the euphoric peak promised by its first glorious 34 seconds.

In bitterly brilliant contrast, Josef K's 'It's Kinda Funny' was a sombre slow dance for syndrum and violin written in the aftershock of Ian Curtis's death, yet simply thrilling in a way that, kind of funnily, 'Simply Thrilled Honey' wasn't. The one-upmanship wasn't lost on Edwyn when they listened to them back on the Dansette at 185. Nor Alan, who thought maybe the rivalry might do Orange Juice some good 'in a Supremes vs. Marvelettes kind of way'. Not that it mattered. Played back to back with The Velvet Underground's benchmark of perfection 'Pale Blue Eyes', thunderstruck by so sobering a contrast, both singles deflated him.

Beyond the battlements of 185, Alan was at least prepared to pretend otherwise. If The Velvet Underground were the greatest band that ever existed, and since it was therefore impossible any Postcard band would ever make a record as good as any of theirs, then it made perfect sense, according to the scam principles and twisted logic of Alan Wild, to promote every one of his bands from now on as the living embodiment of The Velvet Underground.

Their Australian friends 'The Woe-Begones', as Alan had since dubbed them, were now 'the eighties version of the '67 Velvet Underground'. Josef K were similarly 'undoubtedly an eighties version of '68 Velvet Underground'. Which logically left Orange Juice, 'a reincarnation of '69 Velvet Underground'. Postcard Records itself, Alan told the press, hoped 'to update the whole Velvet Underground catalogue for the 1980s'.

Alan had half a heart to keep The Woe-Begones, who still sent letters from Brisbane filling him in on their latest exploits, 'submerging ourselves in midnight rugs and our mother's drugs', their inability to stop 'doing Edwyn and Alan impersonations' to oblivious Aussie friends, and their recruitment of a new permanent drummer called Lindy. But that still left Postcard with only two bands in the northern hemisphere, one of whom Alan didn't even like very much. More out of obligation than pressure, he and Edwyn began sniffing out new blood to pressgang into the kitten's service – preferably those who could be moulded without too great a struggle into one of the few available phases of The Velvet Underground left in Alan's A&R spectrum.

There was now a steady volley of tapes arriving through the 185 letterbox from eager amateurs across the country. None of their trebly twangings made any impression on Alan, who made no effort to hide his indifference in cursory handwritten rejection letters:

Dear beginners, Thanks for sending the tape – wasn't too excited by it to be honest but wouldn't mind hearing any more you do, blah blah, Yours, Alan.

Only one new band, besides Orange Juice, genuinely excited Alan. He'd previously known them as The Dirty Reds, an epilepsy of Edinburgh noise who'd supported Josef K in the dimly lit bat cave of Glasgow's Mars Bar, dodging glass missiles from punk neds as they blitzkreiged on with defiant disregard. They'd since changed their guitarist, their sound to an even shorter, sharper shock and their name to the Fire Engines. Alan was as captivated by the aesthetic appeal of handsome young frontman Davy Henderson as he was by their energy – less a band than an amplified seizure, whose gigs rarely exceeded the 20-minute mark.

Despite his best wooing efforts, the Fire Engines had already made their own plans. A friend of theirs at Edinburgh art school had blown his grant in cahoots with manager 'Angus Groovy' and set up their own label, Codex Communications. It cost them just £36 to record the Fire Engines' debut single in a cottage in the sheep-crofting wilds of Fife, home to Wilf Smarties, an electronics boffin and leader of his own bong-puffing ensemble, Mowgli And The Donuts. Smarties set up the mics, cooked some pizza, and let the tapes capture their mad migraine pop in all its straitjacket-busting glory for the next four hours.

Back across the Forth Road Bridge, Davy played the finished session to his friend Malcolm from Josef K. Malcolm suggested they pick the track 'Discord' as the A-side.

'Discord?' Davy spluttered. 'Malcolm, what ya talkin' about, ya raj? It's crap! What about this one?'

'This one' was 'Get Up And Use Me' and was so much more discordant than 'Discord' it sounded like the public execution of common sense made music.

'What?!' Malcolm laughed. 'Nah! I mean ... no way!'

It was all Davy needed to know they must release it. 'If only to piss off Malc.'

'Get Up And Use Me' was £36-worth of well-spent genius. And proof that by losing the Fire Engines, Alan had lost his eighties version of the Café Bizarre '65 Velvet Underground.

It smarted all the more that he'd already gone and announced the Fire Engines as one of two forthcoming 'new discoveries' on Postcard's latest press release. The other was a band from the Southside of Glasgow called Altered Images. Their singer was 18-year-old Clare Grogan, Steven's record shop admirer of old and one of Edwyn's so-named 'munchkins', forever beaming in the front rows at Orange Juice gigs. Clare worked part-time as a waitress at the Spaghetti Factory, a West End Italian restaurant with a stage at the rear, where Orange Juice would sometimes play to confused diners whose digestion of lasagne wasn't always helped by four fringed spooks dressed like the Von Trapp family singing '*we sit here in torpor*' over out-of-tune guitars. The Spaghetti Factory's resident 'ice cream artiste' was another Postcard associate, photographer Robert Sharp, who in Alan's eyes carried himself like Carmen Ghia from *The Producers*, thus earning him the mischievous Horne handle 'Campo'.

It was while waiting tables there one Halloween, dressed as a Latin American dancer, that Clare met director Bill Forsyth. He asked if she wanted to be in his next film. She thought he was 'just a dirty old git'. Six months later, he came back offering her one of the main love-interest leads in his teenage comedy *Gregory's Girl*. Filmed that summer in Cumbernauld, it wasn't scheduled to be released in cinemas until the new year. In the meantime her career hopes were firmly safety-pinned to the band Alan was already claiming for Postcard.

Edwyn dismissed Altered Images as 'kindergarten Banshees' but was prepared to indulge them thanks to his chronic infatuation with Clare's older sister, Kate. Alan's motives were equally cynical. He knew 'wee Clare' had already quickened the pulse of John Peel at the recent Futurama festival in Leeds. If they joined Postcard, Altered Images were his potential Trojan Horse for increased airplay on the BBC.

Their manager, Gerry, had other ideas. A short meeting in the kitchen boardroom of 185 came to nothing. They wanted to make a record produced by Steve Severin of the Banshees. 'An idiot,' said Edwyn. By Christmas, Altered Images had signed a major deal with Epic Records and got the idiot of their dreams. And with that Alan lost his chance to sign the eighties version of the Mo Tucker-novelty 'I'm Sticking With You' Velvet Underground.*

Much less promising were the efforts of Clare's friend Hodgey, a specky Southside kid in blue-frame glasses, now duffle-coated editor of punk fanzine *The 10 Commandments*,

---

* Clare Grogan disputes that her band were ever in serious consideration for Postcard. 'We got quite friendly with them because we were huge Orange Juice fans and Postcard was really interesting. We loved Josef K. But the weird thing about Altered Images, which pissed a lot of people off, was that from the word go we always said we wanted to sign to a major record label and be really, really popular. We weren't interested in being indie. The Banshees weren't. They were signed to a major, which is what we wanted.' Guitarist Gerry 'Caesar' McNulty remembers otherwise, that he and manager Gerry McElhone, brother of band bassist Johnny, had a meeting on the subject with Alan at 185 West Princes Street.

which he wrote, and photocopied, in spare afternoons at the architects office where he worked. To fill its pages he started making up stories about non-existent local bands, including 'The Oxfam Warriors'. Alan was intrigued by the description and hassled Hodgey to hear a demo. In desperation, Hodgey recorded himself repeating two chords on guitar over a borrowed drum machine, singing lyrics taken from an old interview with Frank Sinatra about the reason he split with Ava Gardner. 'She Hates Travel.'

Alan liked it. He wanted to see The Oxfam Warriors live. Hodgey was stuck until Altered Images' manager, Gerry, recruited a makeshift backing band for him. The lie now a manifest reality, they booked themselves a lunchtime gig at the art school's Victoria Café where Hodgey's cover was finally blown. The Oxfam Warriors were an aptly named charity case, or so Alan and Edwyn thought as they sat at a table near the stage holding up *Juke Box Jury*-style 'HIT' and 'MISS' dummy cards. Mostly 'MISS'.

'Hodgey, your songs are all right,' sighed Alan, 'but your band are a bunch of wee neds.'

It didn't deter Hodgey from continuing his fanzine, finally with enough real bands to write about instead of fake ones and now assisted by Robert Sharp and his girlfriend, writer Kirsty McNeill, who'd both soon spring from the provincial Xerox of *The 10 Commandments* to the national presses of the *NME*.

Nor did it dissuade Hodgey from flapping around 185, brainwashed by Alan's daily Dansette mantras. The same record over and over again, whether a modern fancy like

Buzzcocks' 'Everybody's Happy Nowadays' or *Cut* by The Slits, the Paddy's gold of Sandy Posey, The Temptations' 'Beauty Is Only Skin Deep', Eloise Laws' 'Love Factory' or Alan's ultimate ecstasy, The Lovin' Spoonful's 'Do You Believe In Magic?', leaving it on automatic repeat until every syllable, every semi-quaver, every last zing of John Sebastian's autoharp had been branded to memory.

When not being hypnotised by The Lovin' Spoonful, flinching from Alan's vulture tongue or weeping raw with laughter as it savaged Brian Superstar or some other prey, Hodgey tried to convince Alan about various local bands he thought he should sign. Ones that, unlike his own, he hadn't made up.

The latest were a bunch of teenagers from East Kilbride trying to be Joy Division. The lead track on their demo was called 'Abattoir' and, to Alan's ears, sounded exactly like a bunch of teenagers from East Kilbride trying to be Joy Division. 'Doomeh' rubbish. But their name rang a vague bell. And then he remembered.

It was a few months ago, back in Alan's summer of depression when Malcolm from Josef K rang him up raving about the band he'd just seen support The Teardrop Explodes at Valentino's in Edinburgh. Malcolm had spoken to them backstage where he tried, unsuccessfully, to flog the fresh-faced singer his old amplifier. He also told them they should send a demo to Postcard, which they didn't. Alan had forgotten all about it until the 'Abattoir' demo. The name on the tape was the same band.

'Aztec Camera.'

* * *

At the age of 16, at a time when most teenage guitar players wanted to be Mick Jones from The Clash, Roddy Frame wanted to be 'the guy from *Parky*' – the jazzy fret-tickler in the house band watched by millions every Saturday night on Michael Parkinson's chat show.

Abnormal of mind, abnormal of talent, Roddy took to the guitar like Turner to a canvas, its strings a secret spectrum of light for him to discover infinite colours and shades invisible to the blind fumblings of his pedestrian peers. Poetry spilled whenever his fingertips touched rosewood frets, his every strum a Sibelius symphony, his every pluck a pirouette by Nureyev, playing as if the wind were his pick ups and the stars his amplifier.

The wind was westerly, the stars those that could be seen beyond the sodium glare of Westwood, East Kilbride, one of Glasgow's overspill new towns south of the city. The youngest of four, his father worked by day at the nearby National Engineering Laboratory, and at night singing in local clubs where Roddy accompanied him. By his teens he'd grown big enough to borrow his dad's work-issue N.E.L. branded donkey jacket. Roddy's friends called him 'Little Nell'.

He asked Father Christmas for 'an electric guitar' when he was five. He got his first one when he was nine; it made a great spaceship for his Action Man. Aged 13, punk encouraged him to start playing it properly, incubating in his bedroom, learning Bowie, Dr Feelgood, The Clash and the theme from *Parky* when not reading the existential gospels of Kerouac, Wilson and Sartre. At 14 he joined his first punk band from Govanhill, The Forensics. At 15 he read that Siouxsie & The

Banshees needed a new guitarist after John McKay quit the band mid-tour. He rang up their record company to volunteer his services. They told him he was still too young.

Roddy's stereo world widened when a friend of his dad's, Billy Bain, a former Clyde Valley Stomper who'd played with Lonnie Donegan, taught him some jazz chords. He scraped enough for the deposit on a twelve-string guitar, a big fat semi-acoustic with f-curls 'like the guy from *Parky*'.

He formed his next band at Duncanrig Secondary School, called Neutral Blue, and wrote his first song, 'Roundabout'. His bandmates told him it sounded 'like Elton John'. 'It won't,' he quipped, 'if you play it properly.' They didn't, and Neutral Blue were no more.

With a change of line-up came a change of name, finding inspiration in the psychedelic Merseybeat of his new favourites, The Teardrop Explodes. Roddy took the word 'Camera' from 'Camera, Camera', the B-side of their 'Sleeping Gas' single. He stuck it beside 'Aztec' for no reason other than it sounded good.

The unexotic reality of life in East Kilbride showed in Aztec Camera's earliest songs, sanded against the pebbledash of new-town schemes and flattened in its concrete underpasses, an inhuman pose Roddy was desperate to commit to tape. The budget for their first demo at Sirocco Studio in Kilmarnock only covered a one-way bus fare. After the joyless plod of 'Abattoir' they began the 20-mile journey home on foot. The sight of three trembling urchins with complexions as grey as their guitar cases was enough to stir pity in a disabled driver who pulled up beside them.

'Wit ya doin', lads?'

'Making a record,' sniffed Roddy.

'Aw. Hop in, boys.'

And the cripple drove them home.

They sent a copy of 'Abattoir' to Zoo Records in Liverpool, home to The Teardrop Explodes. They wanted a record deal. They got the next best thing, a support slot on the Edinburgh and Paisley dates of the Teardrops' upcoming tour. The first night at Valentino's on 18 May was the best day of Roddy's life. Or it was up until the moment Teardrops singer Julian Cope told him the news that Ian Curtis had hanged himself. Roddy sat in shock, certainly in no mood to entertain the guy who'd sneaked backstage to try to sell him an amplifier.

He introduced himself as Malcolm from Josef K. He said he'd enjoyed their set and suggested they send a demo to Postcard Records in Glasgow. Roddy said, 'Uh-huh.' He had no intention of doing so.

Roddy had already heard of Postcard after reading a copy of Hodgey's *10 Commandments* fanzine featuring an interview with a band called Orange Juice. At first, he'd seen the photos, with their checked-shirts and big guitars, and assumed they were American. They looked great. Then he read they were from Bearsden in Glasgow.

'Fuckin' poshos!'

The interview also quoted their manager, an opinionated menace who slagged off everything Roddy liked, adding Orange Juice were 'the only band worth seeing'. His name was Alan, head of Postcard Records. Roddy didn't even consider wasting a stamp sending them a demo. These people were, very obviously, monsters.

In the wake of the Teardrops supports, Aztec Camera slowly shed themselves of the stench of the slaughterhouse. Ian Curtis now dead, Roddy had no desire to imitate his tonsils any longer. His words, 'We Could Send Letters', became more romantic. His tunes, 'Just Like Gold', became just that bit more *Parky*. His attitude, sacking his bass player Welshy, more determined.

'You're out,' he told Welshy, 'he's in.'

'He' was Campbell Owens, formerly of local punks The Stilettos. They'd been friends since secondary school, the older Campbell gobsmacked by this precocious spiky-haired Bowie wannabe who could play 'White Riot' better than he could. He was already Roddy's confidante, spending afternoons at the Frame house smoking, talking dreamy existential codswallop, drinking tea and eating plain rolls with St Ivel spread. Campbell was about to leave town for a place at Dundee University when Roddy asked him to join Aztec Camera. He couldn't, and didn't, refuse.

Now galvanized as a trio, with Campbell on bass and drummer Davy Mulholland, Roddy continued saving money to record new demos while writing new songs, still rehearsing the theme from *Parky* and hustling for gigs wherever they could find them.

The Silver Thread, Paisley's old 'Punk Rock Hotel', had since been usurped by a new breezeblock venue called the Bungalow Bar. It was there that Aztec Camera had already supported the Teardrops back in May, and where they were invited back one Tuesday night in late October to open for The Revillos – the contractually renamed reincarnation of Edinburgh's Rezillos, graduates of the Brian Cant school of children's party punk.

Roddy didn't think they'd played an especially brilliant gig so hadn't expected the backstage invasion of well-wishers afterwards. He immediately recognised Malcolm, potentially the world's most persistent amplifier salesman, now flanked by two accomplices for extra muscle. Not that there was a lot of evident muscle in Edwyn and Alan.

'Hi,' said Malcolm. 'This is Edwyn. This is Alan.'

Roddy froze. Edwyn. Alan. It was those horrible bastards he'd read about in Hodgey's fanzine.

He steeled himself ready for the onslaught. Ready to tell them in his fiercest East Kilbride schemie burr that they could take their posey West End Glasgow chic and stick it right—

'That,' Alan interrupted his train of thought, 'was classic.'

Malcolm beamed at Roddy with a 'told you so' smile while Alan looked him up and down.

'Malcolm says you're only sixteen?'

'Uh-huh.'

Alan made a 'fancy that' face at Edwyn, who giggled back at him. Then Alan spoke with an air so casual Roddy wasn't even sure he heard it correctly the first time

'Has anyone ever told you you're the eighties version of sorta supper club *Live At Max's* 1970 Velvet Underground?'

7.

They'd only been on the road for a couple of hours but it was already the worst journey of Alan's life.

It was the end of December, and he was freezing. It was pitch black, and he couldn't see. There was one thin slit for ventilation, and he could barely breathe. And he could barely move, locked in the same gloom with Edwyn, Orange Juice, half of Josef K and all their equipment. It was unbearably grim, and all the more unbearable with every torturous minute that passed knowing he'd have to suffer this all the way from Scotland to Belgium.

Both bands had been booked for a New Year's Eve gig in Brussels. The bright idea to drive everyone there across the ferry in one hired van was the cost-cutting genius of Josef K's manager, Allan Campbell. A fine theory, in principle, providing it wasn't a box-on-wheels Luton van, the kind designed for long-haul furniture removals, reducing any poor creatures who couldn't squeeze into the driver's cabin to illegal immigrant status, rattling in the back of a blacked-out windowless coffin. Which is where Alan now squatted, cabined, cribbed and confined in blindness and misery, quietly taking stock while the hum of motorway traffic droned beyond the walls of his metal prison.

Things were changing in Glasgow. Orange Juice, once the poofy pariahs of beer-sloshing hecklers, now found themselves welcomed. Faces that once sneered from below the stage yelling 'Please finish soon!' now sparkled at them with starry-eyed fancy. The aloof fashion fops last seen pirating around in loose silk and leather, scoffing at Edwyn's checks, now tried to ape his every eccentric stitch in clumsy and conspicuous worship. Where Alan and Edwyn once went to see bands and stood alone like lepers, now the same crew of wretched souls who'd spitefully shunned them rushed to sycophantically bask in their glow. All it took was a few articles in the music press for every Jimmy-come-lately local hipster to beg entry to their gang on jodhpured knee. It was a hilariously weird feeling.

On stage, Orange Juice were still a string-breaking shambles held in place by the sticky tape of Edwyn's comedy – 'Hello, we're Orange Juice … does anybody have a plectrum?' – and James's confusion – 'Are there any Caucasians here tonight?' But their songs were braver and more beautiful than ever. Modern romantics, Edwyn and James wrote as they spoke. Edwyn called James 'You Old Eccentric', James called Edwyn a 'Tender Object', and melody flourished. Immune to Blue Stratos machismo, they sang of chivalry, chastity and the sorrow of '*never being man enough for you*'. Edwyn's heart now thumped to Gershwin, Cole Porter and Noël Coward. James wrote a valentine called 'Wan Light' on the back of a postcard of Lord Byron. Together, they made extravagant work of introspection.

Surrendering to such splendours, John Peel finally caved in and offered them a radio session. It was a major victory for Alan, who likened Peel and his producer John Walters to 'two old maids saying, "We're holding the door to the rock biz and you're not getting in unless you're polite".' Before they travelled down to record it in London, Walters told Orange Juice they'd be better not to bring Alan with them: 'You'll get nowhere in this business with someone like that!'

In search of adventure, David decided to hitch down to the session with their friend Peter, the pair soon finding themselves in the cabin of a manly trucker who, possibly irked by David's delicate frame, launched into a monologue about the world turning soft and the need to bring back National Service.

David listened and smiled before quietly piping up, 'I thought about joining the armed services once.'

'Oh?' said the driver. 'Which one?'

'The Wrens.'

The Peel session had been one of many cheeky cavorts south of the border in the dying months of 1980. There'd been an all-day Manchester festival, 'Dr Fun's Carnival Chance', a fundraiser for local fanzine *City Fun* also featuring The Fall. Singer Mark E. Smith had provisionally agreed to put up Orange Juice in his house. He changed his mind after meeting Alan. 'A weirdo,' recoiled Smith.

There'd been a support to Buzzcocks at the London Lyceum, a trip accompanied by the irrepressible Paul

Naughty heeding a very personal buzz-signal. Pete Shelley, blissfully unaware of their devoted fan's incarceration, had been concerned enough to print 'Where is Paul?' on the sleeve of their new single, 'Strange Thing'. Backstage at the Lyceum, Paul knocked on the Buzzcocks' door and walked in. Which, for reasons Orange Juice couldn't fully eavesdrop in the dressing room next door, ended in a volley of screams and crashing furniture, thus answering Shelley's question.

And there'd been a week in December supporting The Undertones through the parochial English snake pits of skinhead aggro. 'Here now! We'll have none of that,' glowed Edwyn as the bottles hurled around his head like a coconut shy. 'We're from Glasgow and we know how to handle cheeky boys like you!'*

When not earning their rock 'n' roll endurance stripes on stage, Orange Juice were learning how best to drain the batteries of the poor prattlers of the press, a process James found especially trying. His best efforts were the revelation that he didn't 'identify with electronic music cos I once got a shock from a plug', that his ultimate goal was 'to own a truffle farm

---

* The Undertones – or as Edwyn preferred, 'The Underpants' – were profoundly affected by Orange Juice. Guitarist John O'Neill's love for their support band later became a form of Tourette's in press interviews, telling the *NME* Orange Juice were 'the pop group I always wanted The Undertones to be,' and sighing to *Sounds*, 'Do we have to talk about us? I'd much rather talk about Orange Juice.' Their contagious influence, as heard on The Undertones' frothy third album *The Positive Touch*, recorded after that tour and released in May 1981, dismayed the Derry band's biggest fan and original champion, John Peel. 'He said he'd never forgive us,' says James Kirk. 'Because after they'd toured with us they suddenly came back with big guitars and check shirts. "I'll never forgive Orange Juice for ruining The Undertones." That was Peel's quote.'

in France', his belief that 'David Bowie was born in Glasgow' and his spontaneous recitation of Billy Joel's 'It's Still Rock And Roll To Me'. After which he thought it safest to stare at every reporter in a mute stupor, earning the reputation of a young man rumoured to speak only during eclipses of the sun.

Edwyn and Alan were infinitely more comfortable when it came to stupefying journalists with their barefaced arrogance, exquisite wit and puerile hysteria. Together they'd happily trumpet the virtues of 'anti-rock', make scandalous allegations about John Peel or nominate themselves Scotland's answer to 'the Chic Organisation'. If ever bored of interrogation, they'd resort to infantile stupidity. Edwyn was asked if he'd ever been disappointed. 'Yes,' he answered, 'when all the little elves and pixies deserted me during puberty.'

Splashed across the bickering pages of the music weeklies, their silly words, and sillier faces, managed to enrage some of their posier pop cronies. None more so than five north London pompoms called Spandau Ballet, who'd just made the top ten swaddling themselves in tartan plaids like some fiendish aberration of Roxy Music-meets-Harry Lauder. Despite their mock-Scotch pose, the Spands took great exception to the authentic skirls of Orange Juice, 'a dress down group' making 'music for over-21s'. This according to their guitarist, songwriter and former child actor Gary Kemp, aged 21. The same Gary who two schoolgirls thought they spotted being interviewed with Spands singer Tony Hadley in an Edinburgh café. They asked for an autograph, walking away somewhat confused and disappointed with the signatures of an equally puzzled Davy and Ronnie from Josef K.

Grabbing the tartan bull by the horns, Edwyn decided he'd write one of his blazingly brilliant letters to Spandau. Orange Juice, he explained, tried to dress posey but being poor wee boys on the dole they couldn't always afford it. 'But maybe you could tell us where to buy your trendy threads?'

The wealth of press coverage was a triumph for Postcard, Alan now serenaded in black type as a 'supremo', 'maestro' and 'the legendary Alan Horne'. But it was a calamity for Edwyn, returning to Glasgow to find a stiff summons from his local dole office waiting on the doormat. Some envious uncivil servant had seen Edwyn sign on – unmistakable as he was, dressed like a cross between *Just William* and Uncle Sandy from *Champion The Wonder Horse* – recognising him as the same lumberjack dandy splashed across the pages of *Sounds* and the *NME.* Furnished with these and other clippings, not to mention his smug *coup d'état* of a ferric C90 cassette of their recent Peel session, they sat Edwyn down and demanded he explain why, and how, a professional entertainer such as he still dared to drain an income from the nation's taxpayers. Which Edwyn couldn't. His dole was stopped immediately.

Denied his £25-a-week giro, Edwyn now turned to his business partner as sole benefactor. The money they'd so far earned had all gone directly into Alan's bank. Despite registering Postcard Records as a business in February, and a separate 'Postcard Publishing' that Halloween, he still hadn't gotten round to setting up a company account. There were no 'books', only various pieces of paper in the sock drawer in his wardrobe. Nor had he hired any accountant to help, fobbing off all such enquiries with the revelation that Postcard's finances were the strict jurisdiction of the mysterious 'Mr Higgy'.

Any late payments to suppliers or outstanding invoices were diverted to Mr Higgy. Any requests for funds to buy new equipment were forwarded for the scrutiny of Mr Higgy. When Josef K's Davy received an envelope containing just four hundred pound notes, the exact funds he needed to buy his dream bass, it was assumed to be the generosity of Mr Higgy. When Alan took Roddy down to London to buy a new guitar from Denmark Street, it was all thanks to the magnanimity of the benevolent Higgy. And when Edwyn turned to Alan asking for a weekly wage after the severance of his dole, it was Mr Higgy who, after careful consideration, was prepared to go as far as a minimal £20 retainer.

Except that Edwyn knew Mr Higgy lived in Alan's brain. Or as Alan preferred to insist 'under the kitchen sink'.

In public, Edwyn still played along much the same with Alan, teasing him in front of Orange Juice, his latest Alan Wild sketch a 'fatso' frittering away his every sou on his bodyweight in fish suppers. Alan would suffer so much before silencing Edwyn in a flash, either by making uncomfortably crude mimes with a banana or striking him dumb with unrepeatable questions about his mum.

But in private, the joke was now starting to wear thin. Edwyn would sit with Alan in Equi, scraping enough change together for a bowl of minestrone soup, which he'd drown in table parmesan for extra protein, while Alan sat opposite conspicuously consuming another knickerbocker glory.

He tried to highlight Alan's gluttony on the Buzzcocks trip. When Alan stopped at a service station to use the toilet, Edwyn and the incorrigible Paul Naughty sat in the van, thinking it would be hilarious if they ate all Alan's stash of chocolate in a speed-chomping, brown-lipped frenzy before he returned. Alan blew like Krakatoa.

On these and other recent dramas, both Alan and Edwyn ruminated in their wintry claustrophobic carriage to the Continent, until the van stopped, the rear shutter raised and their lungs flooded with a rush of cool air.

They'd arrived at the ferry terminal in Dover for the crossing to Ostend, before the last hour or so in the van to Brussels. The plan was to rendezvous with the other half of Josef K, Paul and Ronnie, neither of whom were prepared to travel refugee-class in a Luton van, least not with Alan, opting to make the journey themselves by train. So they waited. And waited.

Paul and Ronnie never showed. Thinking their train had been delayed, manager Allan Campbell left the passports they'd given him for safe keeping at the ticket office and a message with Malcolm's dad in Edinburgh, praying that when they got to Dover and saw they'd missed them they'd phone home, learn the van had gone ahead, and take the next ferry. It seemed a good contingency plan. And might have worked had Paul and Ronnie not already been arrested as a pair of suspected stowaways.

Earlier that day they'd reached Dover ahead of schedule, waiting for the van long enough to worry whether the combined talent of Postcard Records had suffocated in transit somewhere down the M1. Unless they were already on the ferry.

Paul and Ronnie wandered through customs, searching the parking bay for anything resembling the white box of death. It wasn't there. They headed back to the ferry gates.

'Where do you think you're going?'

The voice honked from under the peaked cap of a border control officer who'd appeared from nowhere to block them with barrel chest and square epaulette shoulders.

'We were just looking for some friends.'

From somewhere beneath the peaked cap two pin-prick eyes scanned them up and down. Paul was pale and East-European thin, looking like some fugitive from Gdańsk who'd fallen from the end of Kafka's pen nib. Ronnie looked even odder, with a bold new haircut, one side short, the other cloaked by a long fringe as if half of his face was poking through curtains.

'Passports, please.'

'Erm, we don't have them,' Ronnie began. 'See, we were gonna meet…'

And so they tried to explain for the next few hours after being frog-marched to a secure interrogation room where, after phone calls to Scotland and the appearance of Lothian constabulary on the doorsteps of the Haig and Torrance households to corroborate their sons' existence, Paul and Ronnie were finally released.

Assuming they'd now missed the van, the ferry and the gig, they caught the next available return train to Edinburgh. Where, having already travelled the best part of a thousand miles with no sleep, their exhausted bodies fell off the train and straight into Malcolm's dad, waiting to pass on the good news: 'You've to turn round and go back to Dover, boys.'

While Paul and Ronnie resigned themselves to a fate seemingly worse than two days locked in the back of a Luton van with Alan Horne, Orange Juice and the remainder of Josef K were testament to the sobering reality that no such fate existed, stepping into the Brussels daylight an anaemic shipment of Scotch veal.

Their destination was Plan K, a converted sugar refinery in the old industrial sector known as 'Little Manchester'. The promoters were two local journalists, Michel and Annik, who'd just set up their own label, Les Disques du Crépuscule (in English, Twilight Records).

Alan took an immediate shine to Annik. She spoke in soft European tones and wore sixties clothes. A potential platonic Nico to his Andy, he'd repeat her name with a tell-tale loving emphasis, 'An-*eek*!' Neither he, nor anyone else around Postcard, had any idea she was the same Annik whose affair with Joy Division's married singer Ian Curtis ended in his suicide and Factory Records' posthumous top 20 hit, 'Love Will Tear Us Apart'. The fact it was the only single from one of Postcard's independent rivals to penetrate the national charts had especially galled Alan. 'We can't all die to get on the radio.' Now here he was, unknowingly charmed by its exotic catalyst.

For Orange Juice, still recovering from their journey, Edwyn already showing early symptoms of cross-channel flu, it was a nightmarish Hogmanay unlike any other: entombed in the warehouse of Plan K, which Michel and Annik had transformed for the night into a five-storey madhouse of illusionism, transvestites, robots, disco dancing, tag wrestling, Mexican food, silent cinema and live bands.

The cocktail of alcohol, guacamole and the sweet sound of Orange Juice sickened the stomachs of one Belgian punk too many, who, incensed by the band's rosy cheeks, runny sinuses and gag tally-hoing, voiced their objections by pogoing to the front of the stage armed with a metal container stolen from the Mexican canteen. Whereupon they hurled its hot, spicy contents with lethal accuracy at Edwyn's head.

Edwyn stood in shock, rice and chilli sauce dripping down his shirt. Then he kicked them in the face with all the force of a penalty shoot-out.

Steven was over the drum kit in a flash, wielding a cymbal stand like a claymore as all Belgian hell broke loose among the crowd.

Such were the state of Belgo–Scotch relations inside Plan K as the prodigal, sleep-deprived, travel-banjaxed Paul and Ronnie finally arrived in Brussels with just enough time for a much-needed restorative meal at a Turkish restaurant around the corner.

Paul and Ronnie spoke no French, nor Turkish. Their waiter understood little English. Even less when delivered with a rolling Edinburgh brogue.

'Just a salad,' said Paul.

'A burger for me,' said Ronnie.

'*Oui, messieurs,*' said the waiter, with an uncertain squint which stayed upon his face all the way to the kitchen.

Twenty famished minutes later he reappeared, minus squint, placing two identical plates under the noses of Paul and Ronnie.

'*Bon appetite, messieurs!*'

Two grey and membranous portions of sheep brains sat atop a smattering of salad leaf.

'Ach, Christ!'

Messieurs made noises not dissimilar to those their dishes would have had they still been connected to the spinal columns of the poor beasts from whence they'd been plucked.

'*Non?*' The squint returned.

'No, no, no.'

Messieurs' plates were taken away, the order repeated, one salad, one burger, the squint now a grimace.

'*Oui, messieurs!*'

Ten weakening hungry minutes passed until he returned.

'*Et voila! Bon appetite, messieurs!*'

The same smattering of salad leaves, the same slivers of sheep brains, this time lodged between a couple of seeded buns.

'Ferfucksakes!'

The grimace became a glower. '*Non?*'

Ronnie despaired. 'For him,' pointing at Paul, 'salad. Just salad. No brains. And just get me a steak. You know, steak?'

The lips said, '*Oui!*', the face, '*Je t'encule.*'

Messieurs' plates were taken away again. Another quarter-hour later the glower stomped back, lobbing a plate of leaves before Paul and a hot, thick, muscly steak under Ronnie. '*Ça va?*'

Ronnie muttered 'aye' while tearing hot flesh, deaf to the grotesque Gallic insults being muttered as the waiter sloped away. He'd barely taken his second bite when Malcolm charged in telling them they had to be on stage. Ronnie tried to wolf his steak down in one. His fork-to-jaw coordination still askew after the journey from hell, he broke his teeth.

Dead beat, malnourished and in dire need of dentistry, Josef K now had to walk on stage before a crowd already rubbed up an infinite number of wrong ways by Orange Juice.

Judging by the dearth of Mexican edibles thrown at Paul's head, the Belgians evidently preferred Josef K. Only a bit too much. The crowd eddied and swirled, a sea of black and midnight hags circling as if around an unseen plughole. It wasn't long before hell resumed as fisticuff flames licked the ceiling. The band were bundled off stage for their own safety. And with that, Josef K's past 48 hours of van asphyxiation, customs grillings, broken teeth and sheep brains reached its aptly depressing anti-climax.

Backstage, Edwyn was still rubbing the smell of food out of his hair when Alan looked at his watch, saw that it was now 1981, and wished him a sarcastic, 'Happy New Year.' Edwyn sneezed a reply.

Alan shook his head and wandered off in search of the fabulous Annik. Edwyn might be sick but it wasn't going to stop him celebrating their first full year of Postcard Records.

Fate's cruel ministers looked down and sniggered. 'The first year of Postcard.' He'd best enjoy himself while he could.

It wouldn't survive a second.

8.

Malcolm couldn't sleep. He wanted to, and, with a studio booked for Josef K the next morning, he needed to. But try as his mind might to knit up its ravelled sleeve of cares and slip away, the voices kept him awake.

One of those voices, the loudest, buzzed through the dark of his bedroom like a euphoric mosquito: 'I found Brian's speed stash. I've taken the lot. I can't sleep.'

Malcolm was well past regretting his offer for Alan to crash in his room at his parents' house the night before the studio. It might have been bearable if Alan had offered to share his plundering of Superstar speed so they could both stay up till the cock crowed, gibbering nonsense. But he hadn't, and so Alan babbled on about hopes and hates, schemes and sins and the next chapter of Postcard to his captive audience of one suffering guitarist.

As part of a company facelift for 1981 they'd adopted a new slogan, 'The Sound of Young Scotland', a knowingly ludicrous homage to Motown, as well as a redesigned record bag, adorned with hand-drawn Victorian scraps of kilted Scottish folk enjoying various 'patriotic' activities copied from an old book Alan had found. 'Redundant Spandau Ballet imagery,' babbled Alan.

He babbled on about Roddy, just turned 17, and Aztec Camera, whose debut single was one of the first of Postcard's new-year crop. 'Just Like Gold' was an urban psychedelic strum about love, loss, diamonds and cigarettes belted out with Aznavour earnest, less a tune than a musical loom woven from the fraying threads of Django Reinhardt and Joaquín Rodrigo. The B-side, 'We Could Send Letters', was a five-minute swoon aching for Eastman Colour and rainy close-ups of Catherine Deneuve like the main theme of a lost Jacques Demy musical. 'It sounds like the Eagles,' Alan had quipped, savouring Roddy's distress for a few seconds before throwing him a lifeline. 'Which is a *good* thing.'

Preciously young, but not so innocent, Roddy had been adopted by Alan and Edwyn, respective crabby stepdad and big brother. Edwyn bedazzled him, an advanced version of himself quarried from the same cliffs of checked shirts, bootlace ties, big guitars, lovelorn lyrics and diminished chords. Except that Edwyn was a West End gent: no drink, no drugs, dreaming tunes in Kelvingrove sunshine. Roddy was a wee schemie from East Kilbride: acid, mushrooms and hallucinating choruses in his Westwood bedroom at four in the morning.

Alan would laugh at Edwyn's tales of taking Roddy to art-school parties and watching him scowl at the bohemian décor, unable to fathom why anyone would decorate their walls with knitting patterns.

Nor did Roddy understand why Alan and Edwyn laughed about eating cheap 'peasant food' in local cafés. 'That's what we eat at home all the fucking time!'

So Alan babbled on.

He kept babbling, about Uncle Geoff, who he still didn't like, not that he needed to as he'd since cracked the code of the workings of Rough Trade.

'Be nice to the secretaries. See, Malc, that's where the gossip is. Uncle Geoff won't tell you anything, but the girls doing the typing – that's where you find out what's really happening.'

He babbled about Orange Juice, whose new single he genuinely hoped might make the national charts. 'With a little bit of pixie luck!' And if it didn't 'the national charts must be done away with!' Both sides were versions of the same flabbergaster, 'Poor Old Soul', an eightsome reel around Studio 54 with a bassline blubblier than the combined effervescence of Chic's champagne fridge. Even the fact that its lyrics, *'the harlequin, the rogue'*, were Edwyn's cheeky elbow in the ribs of his knickerbocker-glory-scoffing business partner – a detail Steven, in particular, enjoyed highlighting in occasional sighs of, 'Alan, you're a poor old soul!' – didn't dampen Alan's enthusiasm.

'It would fit perfectly into the top 30, and at the same time make every other record look sick!'

So Alan babbled on, dawn nearing, Malcolm drooping and drowsing.

He babbled on about his and Edwyn's various Postcard scams, forever finding new ways to amuse themselves and make chumps of the music press.

The Zowie Bowie Scam, in which they successfully conned *Sounds* into believing Postcard had 'signed' David's 10-year-old son, so the yarn spun, after the kid picked up the phone when Alan rang up the Bowie household out of the blue.

The Barry White Scam, in which the press believed Alan's howler that Aztec Camera were going to record their debut album at Sigma Sound in Philadelphia, with Barry producing.

The Sheena Easton Scam, a faint hope their new London ally Grace could put them in touch with her sister's best friend and Glasgow's 'Modern Girl' top ten pop sensation. To 'borrow her' for a Postcard session.

The Oi! Imposter Scam. Using a nearby basement rehearsal room and dingy eight-track studio named the Hellfire Club, Orange Juice toyed with making their own Cockney Rejects spoof to be released under an Oi! band alias to see if anyone took it seriously: they never found the time.

The Joe McKenna Scam, which wasn't so much a scam, more a calamity of camp. An invincibly delicate soul, Joe had grown up in Glasgow, attending the same school as Paul Naughty, but first tasted national fame in the Manchester studios of Granada Television playing Ken Barlow's teenage son, Peter, in *Coronation Street*. By 1981 he was back in Glasgow, an unmissable presence at Orange Juice gigs where he'd sometimes stand at the front screaming 'Steven Daly! Get yer kit aff!', all the while fermenting his own outrageous thoughts of launching a pop career. Which, inevitably, led him skipping up the stairs of 185 West Princes Street for a summit with Alan.

Alan had a lot of time for Joe, not just because his powdery voice and mannerisms made Alan, by comparison, look like your average bricklayer, but because his mingling in exotic circles, including Andy Warhol's goddaughter, was guaranteed quality gossip, turning up at 185 that day having just returned from a Roxy Music album cover shoot in Ireland.

Joe's pitch rested on a scrapbook of garish costume designs for a high concept car crash of music and fashion, the in-no-way pretentious 'A Cha Cha At The Opera'.

'Now then, Alan, I've got the visuals!' enthused Joe, opening his scrapbook. 'It's going to be *veeerry* glamorous! A Cha Cha At The Opera! See, Alan, what I'm trying to combine is *elegance*, which is what the opera is, with something with a bit of *humour*, like the cha cha. What do you think?'

Alan didn't know what to think. Joe persevered.

'So, Alan, I have the visuals, I just need some disco music to go with it. This is where you come in. Alan, you've simply *got* to get Orange Juice to help!'

Amused and a little confused, Alan was prepared to humour Joe, taking him along to the next Orange Juice rehearsal at the Hellfire Club.

'Play me some disco!' Joe encouraged, clapping his hands.

Edwyn obliged, leading David, James and Steven through a spontaneous take-off of Joe Tex's 'Ain't Gonna Bump No More (With No Big Fat Woman)'. The tapes rolling, Joe dived towards the microphone drunk with delight and began shrieking what, to Alan at least, was an incapacitating barrage of absolute nonsense about Robin Hood, poodles and Fred Astaire.

Convinced, nevertheless, that this ramshackle demo would swiftly cha-cha-cha him into the charts, Joe asked Alan to introduce him to some music journalists on his next visit to London. When Alan first called upon him at the Chelsea pad of his friend, 'Lady Natasha', he was greeted by the upper-landing cry 'Come up! I'm in the bath!' and, seconds later, the indelible vision of Joe up to his chin in a sea of bubbles like Joan Crawford in *The Women*. Alan went as far as helping him arrange a first tentative meeting with his friend Sunie at *Record Mirror*. Joe turned up at the agreed place and time, announcing his arrival with a yodel of 'Yoo-hoo!' dressed in a sailor's outfit looking exactly like Tadzio from *Death In Venice*. A good point, Alan decided, to stop trying to make a pop star of Peter Barlow.

The Elton John Scam. In one of his more brazen efforts to land a cash windfall, Alan told David to compose a letter to the former Reg Dwight, along the 'wise up, old man' lines that since he hadn't had a top 40 hit in ages he'd be better off blowing his considerable millions bankrolling superior young talent like Orange Juice. 'And send him a record,' Alan told David. 'Actually, scrap that. Don't waste a record on Elton John. Just send him some photos and say give us some money. That should do the trick.' A week later Elton rang up 185 and Alan all but passed out. Until realising 'Elton' was a mischievous Brian Superstar calling from his work.

And the Paul McCartney Scam. Alan and Edwyn had been listening to 'Silly Love Songs' by Wings on the radio, both agreeing they liked the arrangement. All of a sudden, Alan leapt up and announced they were getting in the car and driving the hundred odd miles to Macca's farm on Mull Of Kintyre. Their mission: to convince the ex-Beatle to produce

Orange Juice. 'He might be reluctant,' Alan admitted cautiously, 'but if that's the case we shall befriend his children. We'll have them convince their father on our behest. We'll be on our best behaviours and do everything in our powers to charm the pants off them. Quickly now, Edwyn! Don't hold the horses, time's a-wastin'!'

They got horribly lost somewhere around Campbeltown, gave up and drove home.

So Alan boiled and bubbled and babbled on to Malcolm in the dead of night, lapsing into impressions of Brian Superstar, Uncle Geoff or spazzing like Bowie's portrayal of *The Elephant Man*, mithering about all the bands he hated, how The Cure, Magazine and Gang Of Four were merely 'this generation's Genesis, Yes and Pink Floyd', and how Postcard's only kindred spirit was Vic Godard. And so on and so on as the slow light of morning crept up behind the curtains.

There'd been another voice in Malcolm's head all night, a quieter one which took over whenever he found rare moments of mental calm, tuning out of Radio Alan. His own voice, wondering how much longer he could trust Alan after the strange series of events to befall Josef K since the clock struck 1981.

Despite the farce of the Plan K gig, Belgium hadn't been a complete disaster. Before returning home, with Orange Juice too ill to take their hosts up on the offer of some free time in the studio once used to voice-over the original Belgian cartoon series *Hergé's Adventures Of Tin Tin*, Josef K obliged. There, in the footsteps of Captain Haddock, they cut the miraculous 'Sorry For Laughing', a funky rumba for handicapped lovers that screamed for release as a single. Michel and Annik wanted it for Les Disques du Crépuscule. Alan agreed that a European import was a 'glamorous' addition to his kitten's catalogue and listed it as a Postcard record in any case.

Foregoing further torture in the Luton van, most of them came back by hovercraft, Paul spending the crossing vomiting into a paper bag. Ronnie, meanwhile, opted for a return ferry crossing so he could smuggle as many cases of Johnnie Walker Red Label back through customs as he could stuff in the band's equipment.

Adding misery to Josef K's ticking time-bombs of Paul's travel sickness and Ronnie's drinking was the disappointment of their proposed debut album, also called *Sorry For Laughing*, scheduled for release that January. They'd produced it themselves with resident Castle Sound engineer Callum Malcolm, a quiet and serious soul whose spirits they attempted to lift with chocolate cream bears. Alan had gone as far as proofing artwork in slick Warhol silver and ordering some white-label test pressings. It didn't sound how anyone had expected. The music was too chocolatey, the mix too creamy and the title track spluttered out of time. It had already cost Rough Trade the handsome sum of £2,000. Alan's verdict was that it was 'as good as Echo & The Bunnymen.' But '*only* as good': he'd never liked the Bunnymen. 'It's not up to Postcard standards.' And so he scrapped it.

As minor consolation, Alan arranged the band's first radio session for John Peel, a 'fake' one concocted from two songs from the abandoned album and two new tracks. Tracks which

Malcolm now faced recording with purple grooves etched under his eyes after a sleepless night with a speeding Alan.

Malcolm's exhaustion was matched in the studio by Paul's grouchiness. It was Alan's idea to use the rest of the Peel broadcast as a preview of their next Postcard single. He'd been pushing hard for them to rerecord 'Chance Meeting', Alan's favourite Josef K song, which they'd never done justice to in its original stumbling keyboard-clopping version for Steven's label. Malcolm's new arrangement was inspired. Much to Alan's delight he'd recently bought an autoharp, just like The Lovin' Spoonful's John Sebastian, using it to zither extra pathos and suspense between its trembling guitars, an epic mood boosted by the marching-band bugling of his 13-year-old brother, Alastair, on trumpet. Except Paul, now 'The Coolest Man In The World' according to their latest review in *Sounds*, wasn't happy. 'I don't even think we should be doing this again,' he harrumphed. 'I don't see why we should.'

Slaughterous thoughts filled Alan's speed-shaken head. Of seizing Paul by the throat with both hands and squeezing until his face flooded a colour worthy of a standardised artist tone somewhere between Primary Magenta and Permanent Mauve as Asphyxiated Maroon. Malcolm could see the murder in Alan's eyes even if Paul couldn't.

'You're doing it,' seethed Alan. No response. He raged on. 'Cos we've paid for this studio. Now fucking get in there and sing!'

Paul scowled back at him, stood up, shuffled into the vocal booth and consigned his twelve lines to tape.

The tenth Postcard single was complete. 'Chance Meeting' was grandiose, poignant and musically electric with summer-seeking lust. And like everything else subject to the acid test of the 185 Dansette: not as good as The Velvet Underground.

But then nothing in Alan's world was or ever would be. Not even, when it happened, an audience with The Velvet Underground.

* * *

Alan and Edwyn's trips to London were no longer epic Jacobite assaults but regular jaunts mixing Postcard business with personal pleasure, which for Alan now meant squeezing in a visit to the sugary paradise of Marine Ices in Chalk Farm. Edwyn had always liked the capital, its parks, its buildings, its funny accents and not-always-so-funny people. He'd once sat on the Tube with James, minding his own blazing business, when a pair of old women with horsey teeth and headmistress tongues piped up at him from across the aisle.

'Hex-kews me, young man, but *what* on earth is *that* hanging out of your pocket?'

Edwyn looked down and saw the raccoon tail of his favourite Davy Crockett hat was poking out of the side of his trousers, from whence he'd stuffed it. He looked up and saw that the horsey women's jackets were encrusted with badges of the Animal Liberation Front. 'A hat,' he said.

'It looks like an animal.'

'Hurgh! It was, but now it's a hat.'

One of the horsey women pulled a face as if someone had broken wind in her opera box. 'Now, what would you say,' she curdled, 'if I walked around with a human skull in my pocket and left the hair trailing out?'

Edwyn replied. 'I'd call you a cannibal.'

Offending people who crossed his path with his blazing big mouth had become an uncontrollable hobby of Edwyn's, but he behaved himself as best he could when it came to meeting the goddess of his teenage dreams.

He'd played Uncle Geoff one of his new songs, 'In A Nutshell', his attempt to capture the more delicate patters of The Velvet Underground with Nico. Uncle Geoff liked it and told him that, contrary to Edwyn's belief that she must still live in an icy penthouse atop New York's Chelsea Hotel, Nico now lived around the corner from Rough Trade in Ladbroke Grove. He could, if Edwyn wanted, organise an introduction through her teenage son, Ari, to play Nico the song and ask if she'd consider recording it. Alan thought this 'the ultimate act of sycophancy' and so the meeting was speedily arranged.

With Ari leading the way, Edwyn, with heart flipping, and Alan, with brain already sketching cover designs for *The Orange Juice & Nico*, followed Uncle Geoff down the steps into a nearby basement flat where daylight dared not shine.

The first thing that struck Edwyn and Alan was the strange, fetid smell. As their eyes adjusted to the gloom, all they could make out were Persian carpets – on the floor, on the walls, on every surface imaginable.

Somewhere in the shadows, a low, slow vampiric voice called out.

'Hell-oooo?'

It hooted like a half-alive owl from a grey tombstone face,

poking into view through a tempest-tossed curtain of black hair. It took a few seconds for Edwyn to realise that this was the same face, once blonde, once beautiful, on the cover of *Chelsea Girl* which his lips had caressed a thousand times.

Nico's eyes settled on Edwyn's face after a lingering glance at his jodhpurs.

'Your trousers,' her voice creaked, like timber in a storm. 'I like them.'

Edwyn trembled a 'thank you', trying and failing to suppress the gleam of shattered illusion in his eyes.

'Do I look like a grandmother?' droned Nico.

'Hurgh! No,' stuttered Edwyn. 'No, no.'

'My son is eighteen,' she smiled at Ari. 'I could be a grandmother.'

And she laughed the laugh of the damned.

Edwyn played her the demo of 'In A Nutshell'. Nico frowned and said she didn't understand the title. Alan knew then that the stars of kitten and banana never would align.

They left Nico's flat confused and disappointed. Edwyn's blazing big mouth triumphed again when he told a journalist friend that his heroine 'looked a little heavy'. They printed it.

A few weeks later the same magazine interviewed Nico. They asked her if she liked any of the 'new breed' of British groups. She admitted 'some of Orange Juice' wasn't bad. 'But I don't like the people at all.'

The curse of Nico upon them, the velvet heart of Postcard was broken in two.

It would never be mended.

9.

There are stories which end in big bangs and swelling crescendos. And there are others which just stop, the projector suddenly running out of film, a blinding white light blaring in the void of a final reel which never comes, while the last dangling frames of celluloid flick around and around.

This is how the story of Postcard ends. Hurtling abruptly into blank.

The last frames flicking around the projector are of Alan. He is in 185 West Princes Street. He is sat in his usual armchair, legs curled up tight against the base. His hands cradle a cup of milk, which he occasionally sips like a kitten from a saucer. A nagging staccato *'ha'* hums from the Dansette. Somewhere, just out of frame, is a curled up copy of a magazine with a quote from Alan Horne on page 26.

'Postcard, in fact, is totally finished.'

Postcard, in fact, is totally finished and Alan is alone, save the voice from the Dansette.

'O mom and dad, mom and dad-a-ha-ha-ha-ha-ha-ha…'

As alone as he ever was five years earlier, a sunburnt 17-year-old in his bedroom in Saltcoats.

* * *

What began with Orange Juice would end with Orange Juice. After four singles, they'd convinced Uncle Geoff they were ready to make an album, with or without Nico. He agreed to fund it, suggesting they record in London, while Alan picked producer Adam Kidron who'd impressed with his work on the Rough Trade debut of melodic Marxist squatters Scritti Politti, albeit a consolatory third choice after higher hopes of John Fogerty and Alex Chilton.

They spent the baking 'Ghost Town' summer of 1981 blistering their fingers and overdubbing brass sections at Regent's Park Studios, Edwyn and Steven lodging in poolside luxury with Adam in Hampstead while James and David dossed down with Babs, a supersized superfan from Los Angeles, now living in Finchley, who'd been trailing them to Scotland and back for the past year. Yet even while they were recording the album, they couldn't help voice their concerns to the press about Postcard's objectives, the national charts, and the chasm between which Rough Trade seemed incapable of bridging.

'There comes a stage when it's just not worthwhile staying on an independent,' blabbed Edwyn. 'We can't reach enough people and we're all completely broke. It's no fun not having any money and being unable to go out.'

Alan didn't argue with them. He couldn't. Pop music was useless unless it was truly populist.

For over a year they'd been talking about 'the One', the big hit which would take Orange Juice, and Postcard, into the top 40. 'Poor Old Soul' was supposed to be the One. Their friends at the *NME* had cooked their books and stuck it in their own version of the chart at number 40, for a laugh. But in the real world it only reached number 80. Orange Juice would never have a hit on Postcard. Edwyn knew it. So did Alan.

With his blessing, their new manager, Mark, began scouting major buyers for the album Rough Trade had already paid for. It was an outright scam and one Alan couldn't resist as a final kick in the seat of Uncle Geoff's loon pants.

The deed was done in the offices of Polydor Records, home of The Jam, Siouxsie & The Banshees and huckle-bucking rockabilly resurrectionists Coast To Coast. Wine was poured as Orange Juice were welcomed by a lawyer who told his favourite story about the momentous day he convinced a reluctant Art Garfunkel to release 'Bright Eyes' as a single.

'And look what happened,' he egged. 'It made Art *millions*!'

Edwyn listened, rocking back in his chair, rocking so hard he flipped and crashed over. James tried so hard not to laugh he turned magenta.

The chair was pulled up, the contract was signed and the rest of the wine was drunk. Nimbly and sweetly it went straight to their heads. They made a toast.

Out of sentiment, it was decided Orange Juice would keep the kitten on the sleeve of their first transitionary single for Polydor. But they were no longer in its clutches.

'Chin, chin!'

Nor Alan's.

* * *

Josef K perished and died that same summer. They'd returned to Belgium to rerecord their album at the same *Tin Tin* studio. At least, second time around, everyone agreed the finished article, in all its sparky urgency, captured their spirit on stage better than the first effort. Everyone apart from the press.

They hated it. Especially Morley, their old ally who'd first described them in the *NME* as 'four shadows', yet for whom *The Only Fun In Town* was 'an artificial paradise totally bungled'. The title and its black and gold picture-book cover echoed the faint laughter beneath their industrial grey, a rarely heard joke they could only properly articulate on stage; sometimes shedding their stereotypical greys for psychedelic shirts and kaftans, or stripped to the waist with war-paint like Apache braves, using pre-recorded tapes to introduce each song, mimicking airport announcements or Frank and Dino routines.

'*Say, did you take a bath this morning?*'

'*Why? Is there one missing?*'

As Alan once mourned, 'No one can see the real Josef K until the raincoats are all put away.' When they'd toured Holland, local promoters listed them as 'depressi-wave'. *The Only Fun In Town* was to be its final ripple.

The month after its release, Paul sat with Ronnie in the Tap O'Lauriston. Despite mixed reviews, the album was selling steadily in the independent charts. Ahead of them lay proposed tour dates in Eastern Europe, and talk of going to America. The future looked golden. It was more travelling than Paul's nervous system could bear. He told Ronnie first. 'I'm leaving the band.'

Ronnie didn't want to carry on without him. Nor did

Malcolm, nor Davy. Two days later, Sunday 23 August 1981, they headlined Maestro's in Glasgow, dressed in black, pallbearers at their own funeral. Davy broke a bass string, which took a lifetime to fix. The mood was subterranean, the sound awful, the regret inevitable. Shakin' Stevens was number one and, by the stroke of midnight, Josef K were no more. They came like shadows, and so departed.

* * *

With Orange Juice gone and Josef K dead, Aztec Camera automatically became Alan's priority. He'd long given up on The Woe-Begones after they sent him a copy of their new single recorded and released in Australia, 'Your Turn, My Turn', asking if he'd put it out on Postcard. Edwyn was there to witness him place it on the Dansette at 185, the disc lasting barely a minute before Alan started fizzing.

'This is *shite!* It's like "Muscle Bound" by Spandau fucking Ballet! They've gone fucking New Romantic!'

Alan's patience with Aztec Camera was only marginally better, as he'd sit in on rehearsals, watching them get to grips with Roddy's latest rococo arrangement.

'Ach, that's dire! You're all over the place. A total *mess.*'

He'd take them for a charitable coffee in the back booth of Equi, trying to ram the absolutist Tao of Horne into their impressionable heads: that they 'knew nothing', that all their favourite bands 'were rubbish' and that, when in doubt, 'it all goes back to Bowie'. They would stare back at him with chalky nicotine faces, their eyes dull through want of vitamins, their bellies meekly content with the shared sandwiches bought with the free luncheon vouchers donated by Roddy's sister. 'My god,' Alan would sigh, sloshing his spoon deep into a knickerbocker glory as they hungrily sucked the steam from their cups. 'You lot are *depressing.*'

By the summer, Aztec Camera were reduced to the duo of Roddy and Campbell, after sacking their drummer, just as Alan was prepared to finance another single, hoping this one may yet manifest his latest fantasy that Roddy could be 'the new David Cassidy'. Unable to find a replacement in time, Steven saved the day, if not the song. 'Mattress Of Wire' was a frisky hare of a tune, its Spanish flutters, Spector steals and sweet farewells to '*ne'er do wells*' sadly handcuffed to the tortoise pace suggested by Orange Juice's new producer, Adam. Backed with the lion-mettled 'Lost Outside The Tunnel', as catalogue number 81–8 it was released that August. The twelfth Postcard record. The unknowing last meow of the kitten.

Roddy still clung on to Alan's promises of Aztec Camera making an album and trying to sell it to a major, just as Orange Juice had done. But with every month that passed, as Alan's bookings became conceptual wine-bar nights playing to only fanzine hipsters and hangers-on, when even Alan stopped turning up to see Aztec Camera play, lamely blaming the icy weather, the grip weakened. Roddy finally saw the light one day in the kitchen of 185, when the phone rang and Alan answered, listened, then snapped 'I'm having my lunch!' before slamming down the receiver.

'Who was that?'

'I dunno,' munched Alan.

Something in the tone of Alan's answer made Roddy suspicious. He pictured some fragrant and tanned chunky-wristwatched London A&R poser swivelling in their leather chair on the top floor of a shiny office block, a major record contract on their desk with the words 'Aztec Camera' pencilled near the top. And their face when Alan rudely hung up on them while 400 miles away, his hopes for Aztec Camera flushed down the toilet of 185 West Princes Street. He tried to ask him again. Alan cut him dead.

'I'm having my bloody lunch!'

Roddy moved to London, where he rang Uncle Geoff, who took great pleasure in signing Aztec Camera to Rough Trade.

Alan stayed in Glasgow and finished his lunch.

* * *

As another golden goose flew from his coup, Alan counted the last of his dwindling Postcard chickens.

His neighbour Malcolm Fisher, the allergic antiquarian pianist, had briefly been a contender after recording some home demos with Edwyn earlier that summer. Roddy and Campbell from Aztec Camera had helped on guitar and bass on the song 'My Guardian Angel', a Bing Crosby-shaped croon cooed with tuxedo elegance by Paul Quinn, Edwyn's school friend from Dundee who'd since been seen modelling Top Man 'Disco Dazzler' clothes in *Jackie* magazine. The quality, that of something recorded on a breadboard during a séance, was too shaky for a single release but good enough to offer to their Belgian friends for a compilation album, appearing under Fisher's chosen name of The French Impressionists.

Alan made a point of name-dropping Fisher's band as his next Postcard project during a TV interview for BBC Scotland's arts series *Spectrum.* The bemused crew lugged their gear up the stairs of 185 West Princes Street to Alan's kitchen where the show's horse-faced presenter, local 'pop star' B. A. Robertson, sat on the sofa beside Edwyn, spluttering in leather trench coat like a drunken junior Gestapo recruit, Alan, tittering in tank top and bow tie like Jerry Lewis's nutty professor, and 185's resident mannequin, all four wearing shades. At the mention of The French Impressionists, the unfortunate B. A. made the dangerous folly of trying to upstage with his Christmas-cracker wit.

'They could record "Give Me Monet" I suppose?'

Alan replied in sub-zero Warhol. 'Oh. Yes. That's. Funny.'

By the time the programme was broadcast, Alan's principal interest in Fisher's band, the voice and face of Paul Quinn, had left. Fisher would eventually find new French Impressionists – 'at a chess tournament, a grouse shoot and an antiques fair' as he'd tell the press – who, no longer of any use to Alan, took their smoky cocktail lounge sweepings elsewhere.

Another of Alan's old friends, polka-dot Jill from the art school, had also formed a new band. Previously Alan had tried to persuade her to start a girl group with his suggested name The Beat Routes. They came to nothing despite help from James, who taught them to play one of his old Nu-Sonics songs, 'Movies' *('Movie-oo-vee-oo-vees!')*. James's influence still shone in Jill's new project with Rose from The Wee Scone Shop, salvaging the name Strawberry Switchblade. They played their first gig at the Spaghetti Factory that Christmas during a winter blizzard. If Alan wanted, he could have signed them. But Postcard was over before the snow had melted.

Hodgey, the one-time Oxfam Warrior and still a 185 kitchen regular, was also making a go of things with his new band, The Bluebells. He took the name from a box of matches, David the teenage drummer from local punks Raw Deal, Russell the guitarist from behind the counter of a record shop, Lawrence the bassist off the street because he liked the cut of his duffle coat, and most of his musical cues from Edwyn: friend, hero and mentor who bounced Hodgey on his knee and christened him 'Bobby Bluebell'.

Alan thought they looked a mess, eyebrows withering over the 'Johnny Rotten shoes' of Ken, David's older brother who joined them on vocals, harmonica and brothel creepers. But he liked their songs. They sounded a bit like The Monkees. So much so, Alan decided they should try and sound even more like The Monkees and write a song as good as 'Last Train To Clarksville'. Hodgey came back the next day with 'Everybody's Somebody's Fool'. The tune was his attempt at a Clarksville rejig with words inspired by Dean Martin's 'Everybody Loves Somebody'. He played it to Alan, who immediately wanted to put it out on Postcard.

'That's a classic, Hodgey!'

Hodgey was thrilled. Until the next day, when he played it to him again.

'That's *terrible*, Hodgey! Stop playing that shit.'

And so Alan turned on his own inscrutable sixpence.

The London music press, still convinced 'the Legendary

Alan Horne' was the new King Midas and Glasgow pop's new Promised Land, gave The Bluebells features without him having to bat an eyelid or them even having to make a record. Such effortless exposure beckoned the offer of a UK tour support for Haircut 100, a band of artificial sprites who'd already driven Alan and Edwyn apoplectic by creating their own London imitation Orange Juice – complete with jodhpurs, knee-socks, semi-acoustic guitars, jangly chords and a fringed-frontman – then audaciously conga-dancing their way to a major deal and the UK top ten. Hodgey thought the tour was the big break The Bluebells needed. Alan told him they weren't ready.

'Fuck that, man,' laughed Hodgey. 'Course we're doing it!'

'Fucking do,' shrieked Alan, 'and don't come back here again!'

The Bluebells did, and Hodgey never came back to 185.

Which left Alan's last resort, another local band jingling sweet jangles about cowboys and Hawaiian moons, who called themselves Jazzateers. Their singer was a waitress called Alison, who looked like a singer and sang like a waitress. Giving Haircut 100 a serious run for their woollens in the Alpine wardrobe department, Alan unveiled them to the press kitted in casual ski-wear – part of his new 'Après-ski' theme, as he'd named a Postcard night at the Spaghetti Factory – prepping them with his pack of lies about how they first met in New York going to see Bowie on stage in *The Elephant Man* and how their guitarist, Ian, earned a crust writing slushy Mills & Boon novels. The press bought it, along with their intentions to release a cover of Donna Summer's 'Wasted', which was true, booking a session with the song's co-writer, Giorgio

Moroder's production partner 'Disco Pete' Bellotte, whom Alan tracked down to a studio in Surrey.

They arrived to find no drum kit. When they asked, Disco Pete laughed and pointed to a drum machine. They had no idea how to program it.

Their bassist Keith, a trainee accountant and possibly the only human being to ever cast a calculation-surrendering eye over the Higgy-ravaged books in Alan's wardrobe, was coaxed by Disco Pete to 'slap' his instrument. Keith wasn't a natural slapper.

Then Alison went in the vocal booth and valiantly honked her best Donna Summer. Disco Pete's face was that of a man who could hear she was a waitress and had already decided against leaving a tip. Having wasted 'Wasted', Jazzateers returned home, where Alison was promptly dismissed and Paul Quinn promptly instated as their new singer. But Jazzateers never did make a record for Postcard. Nor would anyone ever again.

Alan knew from the moment Orange Juice had gone, it was over. Theirs had been the lesson to burst the bubble, leaving him isolated in his own hopeless A&R conundrum corner. He'd been paying for bands to make records to get in the charts. If they were good enough to reach the charts, he could lease them to a major label. If he couldn't find a major label who'd take them, then it wasn't worth releasing them on Postcard because they'd never reach the charts. The fruitless crown of the independent chart, yes, but not the real top 40 of Tony Blackburn, *Top Of The Pops*, 'I'm Still Waiting' and 'Rock Your Baby'. The only chart where life and music mattered.

But how close he'd nearly come.

It was during the summer. Alan first heard it through Rough Trade on an import single on an obscure New York label, One Ten Records. Eight minutes of mesmeric vocal genius.

'Ha ha ha ha ha ha ha ha…'

He'd play it on repeat at 185, the hallway echoing to the robotic stutter, never tiring of its haunting android warmth. As yet the record had no UK distributor. Alan knew it could be a hit and made a bid. He lost out, as did Mute, as did Rough Trade, to the merciless might of Warner Brothers.

'O Superman' by Laurie Anderson reached number two that October. It stayed there for a week before being knocked off by Altered Images' 'Happy Birthday'. Both Postcards that could have been. Both Postcards that never were. Alan had won many battles, but by the first snowfall of winter 1981, the war was lost.

And so, the final frames. Alan sits alone. Just him, and 'O Superman', the last laugh of fate's cruel ministers on his Dansette, and his cup of milk. And no Edwyn to annoy, no Edwyn to amuse. Postcard, in fact, is totally finished. The kitten is gone. The drum is silent. The projector clicks. The film runs out. Our story is done.

But everybody loves a happy ending…

10.

'Oh, boy! Some great music tonight! That was Annie Lennox and Eurythmics. She's from Scotland! And so are *this* lot...'

'Tonight' was Thursday 10 March 1983 and 'this lot' were Orange Juice. But more to the point – and 'oh, boy!' – this was the primetime Petri dish swabbed from the national charts at 7.30 p.m. on BBC1. Eighteen months after the death of Postcard, they'd finally made it to the rainbow's end of *Top Of The Pops.*

Orange Juice, but not quite the same Orange Juice as had once daydreamed of chart glory with Alan around the kitchen table of 185 West Princes Street. It was still Edwyn, singing and giggling in Warhol shades, bootlace tie and biker boots. It was still David, smartly suited, eyes similarly shaded, hand slicing at his bass strings in an unconvincing mime. But it was now Malcolm, not James, on guitar.

Edwyn roped Malcolm in the moment Josef K crumbled, turning Orange Juice very briefly into a five-piece until strange chemistries split them asunder. With the move to Polydor, it was obvious James's oblique oddness, his passive-aggressive tendencies to sabotage gigs by unplugging his guitar and strumming in vacant silence, wasn't built for fame. He was given the boot before their debut album reached the shops. As was Steven, their secret business-brain who'd worked miracles helping negotiate the major contract only to be simultaneously culled, his stool eventually taken by a Zimbabwean drummer from the Glasgow club circuit called Zeke.

The faces had changed, but the spirit of classic Orange Juice was never more sweetly concentrated than on their belated battering ram into the top 40, 'Rip It Up'. Its title was Elvis-via-Little Richard, its sentiment winsome and lovelorn, its groove bumping like Tom Tom Club's 'Genius Of Love', its alarm-bell guitars ringing like Chic, its centrepiece Edwyn's homage to Buzzcocks, quoting 'Boredom' both in 'humdrum' rhyme and nee-nawing guitar solo.

After four previous Polydor flops, Edwyn had all but given up on a hit single. 'Rip It Up' itself was nearly thrown away as a B-side until salvaged as the title track of a contractually rushed and largely ignored second album. Asked by the press to account for the song's eventual success, Edwyn paid his respects to the kitten of yore. 'We've regained something of the old Postcardian positivism.'

That second week in March, Orange Juice were number 22 and climbing; sandwiched, in the countdown, between Wham! and Blancmange, and on *Top Of The Pops* between Eurythmics and the ever-trendy-threaded Spandau Ballet.

A fortnight later, with 'Rip It Up' rising to number nine, they were invited back to capitalise on their victory for a second time. As was custom, *Top Of The Pops* was pre-recorded on a Wednesday for broadcast on the Thursday night. Only this particular week, the Thursday schedule was disrupted by the national *Song For Europe* heat of the Eurovision Song Contest. Meaning *Top Of The Pops* had to go out live, as it happened – whatever happened – on the Wednesday.

The programme's rehearsal regime called for an early start. Orange Juice arrived at BBC Television Centre in various states of bleary grumpiness, with Malcolm and David still speeding from the night before, in no mood for striking up conversation with their fellow guests, including a clatter of half-mast chimney sweeps called JoBoxers and their almost Postcard labelmates Altered Images. Edwyn had also invited along their friend Jim, a musician and producer who made records under the alias You've Got Foetus On Your Breath, thinking it would be a great idea to sneak him on set in the guise of their 'saxophone player'.

They sat in their dressing room waiting for the camera rehearsal, variously speeding up and slowing down in alternate blasts of amphetamine and whisky. Finally ushered on set, Edwyn couldn't help but notice the show's dance troupe, Zoo, on an opposite stage where, with fixed grins and scarlet hotpants, they proceeded to tear scraps of coloured paper while Orange Juice played. Ripping up to 'Rip It Up'.

Edwyn was aghast. He appealed, in vain, to the producers to change their minds. But there was no getting rid of Foxy, her fellow Zoo dancers and their choreographed origami. And so they slouched back to their dressing room, to speed, to whisky and to the girls in make-up who did their best to fulfil David's queer request to make his eyes 'as black as humanly possible'.

At exactly 7.31 p.m., with *A Question Of Sport* finished and the nation spared the witchy cackle of Willy Carson for another week, the 'On Air' light of Studio 7001, TV Centre, glowed red as twelve million viewers tuned in for a rare live *Top Of The Pops.*

First on were the chimney sweeps. Then a clip of David Bowie's new video, 'Let's Dance'. Then the alcohol-and-amphetamine-spiked cocktail called Orange Juice.

Fate decreed that the show's co-host that historic night was the corporation's least enthusiastic Orange Juice fan, John Peel. His encouraging starter pistol: 'Play those ukuleles, boys!'

On the surface, all was calm. Edwyn, looking the consummate professional, mimed in perfect sync. Zeke did a convincing job of pretending to hit his drums. Malcolm swayed in steady time to the beat. The crowd gently bopped. The Zoo dancers commenced their paper-ripping aerobics. And then David lost his mind.

The first verse wasn't over before he grabbed his head as if trying to stop invisible radiowaves infiltrating his skull, the ones telling him to strut and fret around the stage with wobbly-legged stealth searching for an exit, or act playing his bass like an impatient uncle trying to start a lawnmower. When Jim appeared for the saxophone solo – not helping by looking like a man who'd just grabbed forty winks in the BBC skip – David began bumping against him, possibly in an attempt to ferret another helping of speed from his pockets before he fell over. Which is what he did next. Falling off stage, then back on stage, then zigzagging into the drum kit.

The next day Orange Juice were summoned to the Polydor head office where they were told they'd been banned from ever appearing again on *Top Of The Pops.* It had always been their dream to have a hit record. Edwyn's dream, Alan's dream, *the* dream. They'd done it, and undone it, in exceptional style.

* * *

Alan would have been proud of Edwyn's primetime shenanigans had he not been depressed. With Postcard finished, he'd spent the last year focusing all his energies on his 'new Edwyn', the toothsome, quiffsome, soulsome Paul Quinn, recording a whole album with Jazzateers in the hope of attracting major-label investment which never came.

Sick of Glasgow and the ghosts of the past, sick of failure and the ghosts of the present, he'd followed Edwyn to London and Grace's house in Hanover Road, becoming its unshiftable spectre of general annoyance immune to all attempts to exorcise him from the premises. He didn't have a job. He didn't have a plan. He didn't have a care. He only wanted to linger in the corner, an episode of *The Alan Wild Show* on permanent repeat until someone or something put him out of his misery.

That someone was Edwyn. Ever since Alan crash-landed in London he'd been telling him, or trying to, that he could easily start another record label through one of the majors. He was Alan Horne of press legend, 'Postcard supremo', the man who'd discovered Orange Juice, now in the top ten, and Aztec Camera, who'd join them in the charts before the year was out, and The Bluebells, who'd since signed with London

Records. They'd give him his own label tomorrow, and an office, and a car, and a salary, if only he'd pick up the bloody phone and ask. 'No,' Alan sagged with doubt. 'I don't want to.' Which left only one possible resolution.

Brrrrrring! Brrrrrring!

Roger Ames, managing director of London Records, picked up the receiver and was greeted by a nasally Scottish voice buzzing down the line.

'*Is that Roger?*'

'Yes.'

'*Hiiiiya Roger,*' buzzed Edwyn. '*This is Alan Horne. You know, Postcard Records.*'

'Alan! Of course. Yes, hello.'

'*Roger, I was wanting to come in and talk to you about setting up a wee label.*'

'Oh, really?'

'*Yes, Roger. A wee label, part of London Records, but my own thing. I know some weally, weally good bands I'd like to sign, and I think it'd be greeeeat for London.*'

'Really?'

'*Weally,*' wasped Edwyn.

'Well, I'm interested, yes. You should come and pop in for a chat?'

'*That'd be greeeeat, Roger.*'

'Let me just check … next Tuesday? Just before lunch.'

'*Tuesday … um …*'

'Or Thursday?'

'*Actually, Thursday works better for me, Roger. OK. I'll see you then.*'

'Great. See you Thursday. Bye, Alan.'

'Bye, Roger. Bye, bye …' Edwyn hung up the phone.

When he told him what he'd done, Alan wasn't sure whether to believe him.

'No,' he shook his head. 'You didn't. Did you?'

'Yes, I did.' Edwyn looked too proud to be lying. 'I rang him up and he wants you to go in and see him. He wants to talk about giving you your own record label.'

Alan's lips started to twitch. 'So you rang him as me?'

'Yes. *Hiiiya, Roger, this is Alan Horne.*'

Alan grinned. 'And he said yes?'

'Yes.'

'So he's giving me a job without me asking?'

'Hurgh!'

'So…' Alan smiled like a rainbow in the wake of a storm. 'It's a scam!'

'No, it's…' Edwyn stopped, choosing his words carefully. 'Hurgh! It's a scam.'

And for the first time in as long as he could remember Alan laughed till he ached. And Edwyn laughed with him. Both laughing with all their hearts, beating against their ribs like a kitten with a drum.

BOOM! BOOM! BOOM!

Afterword

'So when is your book ending? Just with Postcard? Those were sort of my normal years compared to what came after. Seriously, the real nuttiness was when I went down to London. That's a whole different soap opera of insanity right there. Another story. God! That's a whole other book...'

– ALAN HORNE

Discographies

1. The Complete Postcard Records

All thirteen-and-a-half of them.

November 1979

WISH001 Orange Juice – 'Felicity'

Written by James Kirk. Recorded live at Teviot Row, Edinburgh on 21 April 1979 by Malcolm Ross.

One-track 33⅓ rpm 'I Wish I Was A Postcard' flexi-disc. Label centre featuring the full Louis Wain musical kittens illustration. Two thousand five hundred copies pressed, intended as a free gift with the aborted fanzine *Strawberry Switchblade*. Instead included as an extra with 'Falling And Laughing'. Remaining copies were given away with various fanzines: Glasgow's *The 10 Commandments* (issue five, Orange Juice on the cover), *The Circus Dream* from Saltash in Cornwall, and with the A6-sized Orange Juice/ Josef K 'bandzine' distributed by superfan Barbara Shores from Finchley, London.

The 'WISH' catalogue number doesn't feature on the flexi itself but was listed in the 1980 *Small Labels Catalogue* along with two other apocryphal flexis.

The first, WISH002, was to be 'Miniature Dogs' by Dave The Rave. Dave was a friend from the art school who came round to 185 West Princes Street one day 'to make a record'. Deciding it should be a rap, Alan asked Edwyn to play the bass line of The Sugarhill Gang's 'Rapper's Delight' and handed Dave various magazines and books, including David Storey's *This Sporting Life*, to freestyle over the top. The title came from a strange back page advert of an old comic: 'For just one penny I will send you a brand new miniature dog'.

The second, WISH003, was 'The Day I Went Down To Texas' by Jake Black, another local punk singer and frequent visitor to 185 with his friend, Parky. A fixture of early Orange Juice sets, the song was later recorded for *Ostrich Churchyard*, listed as 'Texas Fever (The Same Symphony)'; confusingly, 'The Day I Went Down To Texas' is also the title of a later, unrelated, Orange Juice song from 1984's *Texas Fever*.

February 1980

80-1 ***ORANGE JUICE – 'Falling And Laughing' b/w 'Moscow Olympics'*/'Moscow'****

*Written by Edwyn Collins and *James Kirk. Recorded by John McLarty with 'production assistance' from Malcolm Ross at Emblem Studios, Strathaven, December 1979.*

The first Postcard Record: 'c/o Alan Horne 185 West Princes St 2/R Glasgow G4'. Blue disc labels featured a prototype of the Louis Wain kitten logo copied by Edwyn. The sleeve, designed by David, was a three-quarter-length wrap-around with a photo of Edwyn, James and David taken by Peter McArthur (uncredited). Alan is listed as 'Alan Wild' for his 'vocals' on the B-side. Initial copies also contained the 'Felicity' flexi-disc and a plain postcard overprinted with the kitten logo. The artwork was printed up first: after picking up the vinyl shipment from the London docks, Alan and the band spent a day in a cheap hotel in Sussex Gardens assembling the sleeves and records together. Officially, a total of 963 were pressed, making it the most sought after and expensive Postcard record for collectors. In a 1981 interview with Glasgow's *Born Yesterday* fanzine, Steven Daly joked, 'We're pressing up another five hundred and selling them at five pounds each.'

Run-out grooves – A: 'Things are tough.' B: 'We can still picnic.' (Lyrics from Vic Godard and Subway Sect's then-unreleased 'Stool Pigeon'; Alan and Edwyn knew the song from a 1978 John Peel session.)

August 1980

80-2 ***ORANGE JUICE – 'Blue Boy' b/w 'Lovesick'***
Written by Edwyn Collins. Produced by Alex Fergusson and Orange Juice, engineered by Callum Malcolm at Castle Sound Studio, Edinburgh on 30 April 1980. Additional organ by Alex Fergusson.
First edition of 2,086 with blue disc labels in a hand-coloured reversible sleeve shared with Josef K's 'Radio Drill Time'. Orange Juice side designed by 'Sharon Acker' (Robbie Kelly, Postcard friend and graphic designer, using the pseudonym of the Hollywood actress best known for *Point Blank* and various TV cameos).

After securing Rough Trade distribution, the next pressings became the first Postcard release to use the cowboy design sleeve: originally white with white A-side and yellow and red B-side disc labels, later issued in brown sleeve and labels. Both featured a Robert Sharp photo of Edwyn with his guitar on side A, taken in a small park close to 185 West Princes Street in July 1980. An

Australian version of the single was later licensed to Gap Records.

'Blue Boy' dates back to The Nu-Sonics, written in 1977 after Edwyn met Buzzcocks' Pete Shelley backstage in Edinburgh on the White Riot tour. The original draft of the lyrics mentioned Shelley's pink '*Sta-Prest*' trousers, later changed to gabardine 'because it scanned better'. Edwyn admits he took the '*curse*' and '*bless*' from Dylan Thomas's poem 'Do Not Go Gentle Into That Good Night'. 'The lyrics are kind of crap,' laughs Edwyn. 'The record's good but the words are kind of back-of-the-envelope type stuff.'

Run-out grooves – A: 'When is an artist at his most dangerous?' B: 'When he's drawing a gun.'

80-3 JOSEF K – 'Radio Drill Time'* b/w 'Crazy To Exist'

*Written by *Haig/Ross and Haig. Produced by Josef K. A-side engineered by Callum Malcolm at Castle Sound Studio, Edinburgh on 30 April 1980. B-side recorded 'live' by Wilf Smarties in Fife.*

As with Orange Juice's 'Blue Boy', first copies came in a hand-coloured reversible sleeve. Josef K side designed by 'Barbara Hale' (Robbie Kelly, this time using the pseudonym of the Hollywood actress best known for her role in TV's *Perry Mason*). The reverse group photo was taken after hours in the Brian Drumm hair salon on George

Street in Edinburgh where Ron Torrance worked at the time.

Later issued in white, then brown, cowboy sleeves. Side A featured group head-shots by Robert Sharp, taken in the dressing room of the Bungalow Bar, Paisley, in August 1980.

The words of 'Radio Drill Time' were inspired by the sleeve notes of Lou Reed's *Metal Machine Music*: 'The records were letters. Real letters from me to certain other people.' A rumour that Grace Jones planned to cover the song has its basis in the fact Rough Trade sent a copy to her management, then in the process of choosing material for what became 1981's *Nightclubbing*.

'Crazy To Exist' was recorded 'live' in the same Fife cottage where Wilf Smarties later produced the Fire Engines' debut 'Get Up And Use Me'. During the session they were called to help Wilf chase sheep out of his garden. Malcolm reasonably suspects that Paul's lyrics about '*shadowed coaches*' and '*sleeping in doorways*' may have been inspired by their miserable London trip to see Joy Division that February.

Run-out grooves – A: 'Malcolm's in luv.' (Referring to Malcolm Ross's girlfriend and future wife Susan, or 'Syuzen', Buckley. 'That's when he met Susan,' confirms Paul Haig. 'They used to throw sweeties to each other in the Tap O'Lauriston. All very innocent courting.')

November 1980

80-4 ***THE GO-BETWEENS – 'I Need Two Heads' b/w 'Stop Before You Say It'***

Written by Forster/McLennan. Produced by Alex Fergusson, engineered by Callum Malcolm at Castle Sound Studio, Edinburgh on 28 April 1980. Drums by Steven Daly.

First issued in white, then brown, cowboy bag and disc labels. A-side featured portrait of Robert Forster and Grant McLennan taken by Harry Papadopoulos at 185 West Princes Street. The single was later licensed to Australia's Missing Link label (MISS23) in a picture sleeve, the cover a drawing of a giraffe in an old abbey.

Run-out grooves – A: 'Hello, Campo you pesky queer.' ('Campo' was Alan's joke nickname for Postcard photographer Robert Sharp, the boyfriend of writer Kirsty McNeill. As mentioned elsewhere in this book, for whatever reason Robert reminded Alan, if nobody else, of Carmen Ghia from *The Producers*.) B: 'Please come back to Glasgow soon.'

80-5 ***JOSEF K – 'It's Kinda Funny' b/w 'Final Request'***

Written by Paul Haig. Produced by Josef K, engineered by Callum Malcolm at Castle Sound Studio, Edinburgh, October 1980. Additional violin, piano and syndrum by Malcolm Ross.

Brown cowboy bag and disc labels, A-side with hazy group portrait taken in London by Harry Papadopoulos. First 5,000 copies in sealable polythene bag with colour photocopied insert of alternative sleeve featuring another Papadopoulos shot of the band chasing pigeons and, on the reverse, four separate Polaroid portraits by Robert Sharp at his flat on Sauchiehall Street. 'The Polaroids are SX-70,' says Robert, 'which at that time had soft emulsion that could be manipulated by surface pressure, just after exposure; later versions of the film were less malleable. I asked each member of the band to manipulate their respective Polaroid, having shown them the technique. This was a homage/reference to the early 1970s work of Lucas Samaras. In those days, the cost of colour printing was a fair consideration, high-quality short-run being relatively pricey. Hence, the inserts were colour photocopies, then a new thing, the limitations of which were apparent, but workable.' One of two Postcard singles licensed at the time in Japan.

Run-out grooves – A: 'S-u-s-a-n.' (Susan Buckley: see notes to 'Radio Drill Time') B: 'Punk Rock.'

80-6 ***ORANGE JUICE – 'Simply Thrilled Honey' b/w 'Breakfast Time'***

Written by Edwyn Collins. Produced by Malcolm Ross and Orange Juice, engineered by Callum

Malcolm at Castle Sound Studio, Edinburgh, October 1980. Additional synthesizer and piano by Malcolm Ross.

Brown cowboy bag and disc labels, A-side with group head-shots by Robert Sharp taken at 185 West Princes Street. First 5,000 copies in sealable polythene bag with double-sided insert as substitute sleeve. According to Peter McArthur, the main cover was originally going to be a photo of Jill Bryson; she appears instead in the bottom right of the insert reverse.

James Kirk agrees that the A-side fell short of expectations: 'In a lot of ways, "Simply Thrilled Honey" used to be my favourite one. We used to play it live and it was like "Be My Baby" and then I'd come in with the big guitar bit and it went right out there. So it was a real shame that didn't come through on the record. The beat was way out, something was wrong.'

Edwyn later explained the meaning of the song to *Sounds*. 'It's about a girl who tried to seduce me, but I didn't want to go to bed with her … that's what the line "*worldliness must keep apart from me*" means. I was simply thrilled, ha, ha, ha! Thanks, but no thanks. I find going to bed with somebody you don't love disorientating.'

'Breakfast Time, Breakfast Time' (its full title, not used on the label) had originally been considered for the reverse of 'Blue Boy'. Here, its B-side status is crossed out on the label with a handwritten 'A' to suggest an unlikely double A-side. The single was provisionally announced in the summer 1980 *Small Labels Catalogue* as being Postcard number 80-5 (eventually taken by 'It's Kinda Funny') backed with 'Upwards And Onwards', one of Orange Juice's best songs, sadly never recorded for Postcard. As with Josef K's 'It's Kinda Funny' this single was also licensed at the time in Japan.

Run-out grooves – A: 'Commercial.' B: 'Progressive.' (A reference to the *NME*'s October 1980 Postcard feature by Paul Morley: 'Horne bemoans the chasm that has developed between "commercial" and "progressive" post-punk music.')

January 1981

81-1 ***JOSEF K* – Sorry For Laughing**
Side 1: *'Fun 'N' Frenzy', 'Heads Watch', 'Drone', 'Sense Of Guilt'*, 'Art Of Things', 'Crazy To Exist'*
Side 2: *'Citizens', 'Variation Of Scene'*, 'Terry's Show Lies', 'No Glory', 'Endless Soul'*, 'Sorry For Laughing'**
*All songs by Haig except *by Haig/Ross. Produced by Josef K, engineered by Callum Malcolm at Castle Sound Studio, Edinburgh, November 1980.*
Intended as Josef K's debut album and pressed up as a limited white-label but never commercially

released. Album artwork was designed and proofed featuring a solarised group portrait taken on Edinburgh's Calton Hill by Robert Sharp, printed in silver pantone with lettering by Krysia Klasicki.

'When we finished the album, we agreed we wouldn't listen to it much because by the time it came out we'd be sick of it,' says Malcolm. 'Then when we did get the test pressings Alan sowed the seeds of doubt, I would say. But we'd moved on a bit and written new songs by then. We just knew the album wasn't as good as it could be.'

'Sense Of Guilt' was the retitled 'Helen Scott' (aka 'The Thoughts Of Helen Scott's Last Boyfriend'). 'Art Of Things' would later be re-recorded for the reverse of 'Chance Meeting' as 'Pictures (Of Cindy)'. 'Citizens' and 'Drone' would be rerecorded with different tunes on *The Only Fun In Town* (the latter retitled 'Forever Drone'). All tracks since released posthumously on various reissues. LTM Recordings issued a vinyl facsimile of the proposed Postcard original in 2013.

March 1981

81-2 ***ORANGE JUICE – 'Poor Old Soul'***
b/w 'Poor Old Soul Pt. 2'
Written by Edwyn Collins. Produced by Orange Juice, engineered by Callum Malcolm at Castle Sound Studio, Edinburgh in January 1981.

The last of Orange Juice's four Postcard singles and the first appearance of the new black Scottish design sleeve by Krysia Klasicki, the reverse with label discography listing the next four scheduled singles, including the intended 'Wan Light'.

Pink disc label with illustration of a child staring at a record on the B-side. First 10,000 copies came with postcard insert with handwritten lyrics and cat cartoon designed by Edwyn.

Edwyn has never made a secret of the song's lyrical debt to Noël Coward's 'Parisian Pierrot' (Coward's rhyming of '*much in vogue*' with '*harlequin, a rogue*').

David and Edwyn swapped instruments for the 'Pt. 2' B-side (Edwyn's bass playing is the more aggressive, though as David states 'there's not much between them'). In an earlier version of the song recorded for John Peel, the chant '*no more rock 'n' roll for you*' had originally been '*new day fashion same old grey*', a lyric from James's old Nu-Sonics song 'London Weekend'. According to Edwyn the clip of screaming fans at the end of 'Pt. 2' is taken 'from a bootleg Beatles live album … I think.'

Run-out groove – B: 'The Message.'

81-3 ***AZTEC CAMERA – 'Just Like Gold'***
b/w 'We Could Send Letters'
Written by Roddy Frame. Produced and engineered by Callum Malcolm at Castle Sound

Studio, Edinburgh, January 1981. Additional help and autoharp by Malcolm Ross.
Scottish design sleeve, blue disc with picture of dancing children on side B. First copies came with postcard insert with handwritten lyrics and group portrait by Robert Sharp, taken near Temple Cottage, Balmore, a hamlet north of Glasgow. Once a hippy, folky haven, its grounds can be seen on the sleeve of The Incredible String Band's 1968 album *The Hangman's Beautiful Daughter*. Roddy is wearing his father's 'Little Nell' works jacket. The Alsatian in the foreground was called Jody and belonged to Temple Cottage's Mary Stewart, a New York beatnik who first settled in the area in the 1950s. 'Robert knew these people, just on the outskirts of Glasgow,' remembers Roddy. 'We went there and all the doors were open. There were prayer mats everywhere and a little Buddhist shrine. It was completely Bohemian in a really cool way. I remember Robert telling us it was where the first acid bust in Scotland was in the late sixties.'

Speaking to Kirsty McNeill in the *NME*, Roddy expressed great pride in his choice of debut single. 'I don't think I could improve "Just Like Gold" in any way. I spent a long time trying to sound un-clichéd. There's no chorus in it, nothing's repeated.'

A different version of 'We Could Send Letters' had already been demoed at Emblem in Strathaven and included on the *NME*'s *C81* cassette. The song was later rerecorded for Aztec Camera's 1983 Rough Trade debut, *High Land, Hard Rain*. Roddy explained the song to *Melody Maker* that year: 'It's meant to be sarcastic. Looking at that position of being so close yet far away. Actually being in the same room as somebody, but the only way you can communicate is to write it down.'

No run-out groove messages.

81-4 ***JOSEF K – 'Sorry For Laughing'****
b/w 'Révélation'

*Written by *Haig/Ross and Haig. Produced by Josef K, engineered by Marc François at Little Big One, Brussels on 2 January 1981.*

Released by Belgium's Les Disques du Crépuscule in a colour picture sleeve with a cartoon of the band by Benoît Hennebert, catalogue number TWI 023. Prior to the Brussels trip which instigated this recording, Alan had scheduled '81-4' as the new 'Chance Meeting'. Neither the word 'Postcard' nor '81-4' appear anywhere on this release, nor the kitten logo; in its place is a very bad drawing of a cat with a drum on the label B-side.

Paul Haig on the lyrics: 'The Charles Atlas reference is about me being thin and the whole song is about a relationship between two people who are disabled and the fun that they have together. They're laughing at the world and they're laughing at everyone else because they're thinking, "They're looking at us and they think we are weird and strange and different." It's about two people having a great wonderful relationship and laughing to themselves.'

No run-out groove messages.

June 1981

81-5 ***JOSEF K – 'Chance Meeting'****
b/w 'Pictures (Of Cindy)'
*Written by *Haig/Ross and Haig. Produced by Josef K, engineered by Callum Malcolm at Castle Sound Studio, Edinburgh, March 1981. Trumpet by Alastair Ross.*

Last of the Scottish design sleeve singles. Green disc label with Harry Papadopoulos band photo (Paul Haig enjoying the Cossack) on A-side. The B-side is mislabelled as 'A', the song listed only as 'Pictures' and mixing up the 'Chance Meeting' composer credit.

It was Josef K's second version of the song, first issued as their 1979 debut on Steven Daly's Absolute label. 'Alan had kind of persuaded us to rerecord our first single,' says Malcolm. 'He thought it had potential and it ended up being our most commercial. Paul was in a huff in the studio and I was running around putting down all these guitar parts and my wee brother was there on trumpet. We double-tracked him to try to make it sound like a full brass section.'

First copies came with postcard insert with handwritten lyrics and a black and white photograph: not of Josef K but a large litter of African wild dog pups. The image was chosen by Alan, sourced from Robert Sharp's copy of the 1977 book *Savage Paradise* by Dutch wildlife photographer Hugo van Lawick.

Run-out groove – B: 'Hello Karl Rossmann.' (The central character in *Amerika*, Paul Haig's favourite Franz Kafka novel at the time.)

July 1981

81-7 ***JOSEF K* – The Only Fun In Town**
Side 1: *'Fun 'N' Frenzy', 'Revelation', 'Crazy To Exist', 'It's Kinda Funny', 'The Angle'***
Side 2: *'Forever Drone', 'Heart Of Song'*, *'16 Years', 'Citizens', 'Sorry For Laughing'*****
*All songs by Haig except *by Haig/Ross. Produced by Josef K and Marc François at Little Big One, Brussels, April 1981.*
The only LP ever released on Postcard, Josef K's rerecorded debut album after the earlier *Sorry For Laughing* (81-1) was shelved. 'We purposely tried to go against the first version of the album,' says Paul. 'We wanted it to sound more immediate

and live, and I mixed down my vocals purposely. I don't know why I did that.'

Black and gold sleeve designed by Krysia Klasicki after Czech illustrator Miroslav Sasek's 1961 picture book *This Is Edinburgh*. No information on back sleeve. Black and gold disc labels.

Inner bag featuring lyrics and collage assembled by Susan Buckley. Images include: various family photos (Malcolm's father, Davy's father with pipe, Paul's mother doing her hair); the Fire Engines' Davy Henderson and friends in the Wig & Pen; a blurry Alan Horne with Les Disques du Crépuscule's Michel Duval; archive photos of Josef K by Peter McArthur and Robert Sharp; a men's clothing advert from an issue of *Playboy* (the magazine logo had been covered up but it fell off before reproduction); Patrick McGoohan in *The Prisoner*; and a television still of the shower scene in Hitchcock's *Psycho* (also by Robert Sharp).

Some of the songs had previously been recorded in radically different versions: 'Citizens' and 'Forever Drone' (formerly just 'Drone') had the same lyrics but entirely new music to those on the unreleased *Sorry For Laughing* while 'Heart Of Song' was a new arrangement of 'Radio Drill Time'.

No run-out groove messages.

August 1981

81-8 ***AZTEC CAMERA – 'Mattress Of Wire'***
b/w 'Lost Outside The Tunnel'
Written by Roddy Frame. Produced by Adam Kidron, engineered by Callum Malcolm at Castle Sound Studio, Edinburgh, June 1981. Drums by Steven Daly.

The last Postcard record. Yellow disc labels with hand-drawn tartan pattern. Dispensing with the recent Scottish design, it came in its own bespoke picture sleeve: a picture of an androgynous ancient Roman with laurel crown sourced from Roddy's grandmother's *Collins Encyclopaedia*. 'When my granny died we took it out of her house and I saw that picture and I said, "Aw, I love that, man. I'd love that on the sleeve." I took it to Alan, thinking he was gonna say, "Naw, it must be cowboys and little boys in kilts." And he said, "Aw, yeah that's really cool, let's stick that on the sleeve." I couldn't believe you could just take something from your grandmother's encyclopaedia and put it on the market.'

Since Aztec Camera were between drummers, Steven Daly stood in, thus spookily completing a Postcard circle, drumming on the label's last release, just as he drummed on its first.

In subsequent interviews Roddy was quick to express his unhappiness with the single, lamenting it failed to capture the song as he'd hoped. Though he would play 'Mattress Of Wire' live, he never recorded it to his satisfaction. The lyrics are notable for a conspicuous homage to Ike & Tina Turner's 'River Deep – Mountain High'.

'Lost Outside The Tunnel' dated back to Roddy's earlier band, Neutral Blue, his attempt to write something along the lines of 'the Liverpool sound' of The Teardrop Explodes and Echo & The Bunnymen. It was later rerecorded for 1983's *High Land, Hard Rain*.

No run-out groove messages.

2. Apocryphal Postcards

Assigned catalogue numbers that were never released.

81-3 ***AZTEC CAMERA – 'Green Jacket Grey' b/w 'Real Tears'***

Listed in the Rough Trade catalogue compiled at the end of 1980. Both had been early Aztec Camera demos recorded prior to Postcard. Number 81–3 instead became 'Just Like Gold'.

81-5 ***ORANGE JUICE – Ostrich Churchyard***

Listed in the Rough Trade catalogue compiled at the end of 1980. Recorded as a 'demo album' in May 1981 at the Hellfire Club in Glasgow with engineer Davy Henderson, it was released posthumously when Alan relaunched Postcard in the early 1990s (see Related Releases).

81-6 ***ORANGE JUICE – 'Wan Light' b/w 'You Old Eccentric'***

The most famous apocryphal Postcard single, listed on the back of the Scottish design sleeve, coupling two James Kirk songs. In later interviews of the period, a rerecording of James's 'Felicity' is mentioned as the proposed B-side instead.

As mentioned, James wrote the lyrics for 'Wan Light' – as in pale light, not the phonetic Glaswegian 'one light' as sometimes assumed – on the back of a Byron postcard from the National Portrait Gallery. 'I wasn't particularly confident about the song,' says James. 'There was a guy called Angus Cook, who used to watch us play the Bungalow Bar in Paisley. Years later he became Cerith Wyn Evans' boyfriend and a model for Lucian Freud. He wore black nail varnish and looked a bit like Anthony Blanche in *Brideshead Revisited*. Anyway, I think he was the one who told Alan it should be a single. We'd already recorded a version for the BBC and somebody said it sounded oriental. With hindsight I got the lyric wrong. It should have been, "*In wooded glades on my trusted steed, air rushing through the trees.*" I'd used the word "*through*" twice, which is really bad.'

The song later appeared as an album track on *You Can't Hide Your Love Forever*. 'You Old Eccentric' became the B-side of Polydor's 'Felicity' twelve-inch (see Related Releases).

81-9 ***THE GO-BETWEENS – 'Your Turn, My Turn'***
Listed in the 1981 *Independent Labels Catalogue*. First issued in July 1981 on Melbourne's Missing Link label, the band had hoped Postcard would issue a UK equivalent. The song was later included on their 1982 Rough Trade debut album, *Send Me A Lullaby*.

81-10 ***ORANGE JUICE* – You Can't Hide Your Love Forever**

Listed in the 1981 *Independent Labels Catalogue*. Funded by Rough Trade, who intended to distribute the album, but released instead on Polydor in February 1982 (see Related Releases).

81-11 ***THE SECRET GOLDFISH – 'Hey Mister'***

An apocryphal release by an apocryphal group, The Secret Goldfish were born of 'jocular' discussion between Edwyn and Malcolm Ross, taking their name from J. D. Salinger's *The Catcher In The Rye*. Before selling-out to Hollywood, Holden Caulfield's older brother, D. B., wrote short stories including Holden's favourite, 'The Secret Goldfish', about 'this little kid that wouldn't let anybody look at his goldfish because he'd bought it with his own money'.

'It was a splinter group that never really went anywhere,' says Edwyn. 'A kind of Everly Brothers thing with acoustic guitars. The song "Louise Louise", an early Orange Juice ballad that eventually ended up on *Rip It Up*, was originally going to be a Secret Goldfish tune too.'

'Hey Mister' was one of Alan's favourite songs by beehived American sixties country-pop tragedian Sandy Posey. Written by Dan Penn and Spooner Oldham, it tells of a poor country girl used and abused in the big city, left begging for the '*one thin dime*' to call her mother back home in Carolina.

In February 1982, Jazzateers supported Aztec Camera at London's King College, listed on the bill as 'The Secret Goldfish'. They later recorded their own version of 'Hey Mister' with Paul Quinn.

81-12 ***THE BLUEBELLS – 'Everybody's Somebody's Fool'***

Also listed in the 1981 *Independent Labels Catalogue*. The song was first released on London Records as a B-side of The Bluebells' 1982 debut single 'Forevermore', produced by Elvis Costello. A rerecorded version opened the band's only album, 1984's *Sisters*.

81-13 ***AZTEC CAMERA* – Green Jacket Grey**

Sometimes referred to as the 'lost' Aztec Camera debut album but never recorded. The title track had previously been muted as their first Postcard single instead of 'Just Like Gold'. Demos, and live versions, of 'Green Jacket Grey' and other early Roddy songs such as 'Remember The Docks' and 'The Spirit Shows' can be found on various bootlegs.

81-14 ***JAZZATEERS – 'Wasted'***

The planned Donna Summer cover to be produced by Pete Bellotte, the song's co-writer who recorded the original with Giorgio Moroder for 1976's *A Love Trilogy*. Jazzateers recorded another version of the song produced by Edwyn, one of several unreleased demos featuring original singer Alison Gourlay.

After Paul Quinn replaced Gourlay, in 1982 the band recorded a whole album mixing originals with covers (including 'Hey Mister' and Mike Nesmith's 'Different Drum'), sometimes referred to as '*Lee*' – erroneously so according to bassist and songwriter Keith Band – as well as a 'lost' Postcard album. In truth, it was always Alan's intention to licence it to a major label. According to Band, Les Disques du Crépuscule's Michel Duval offered to issue it posthumously. Alan refused, joking that he couldn't release it since 'it wasn't as good' as 'White Lines (Don't Do It)' by Grandmaster & Melle Mel.

3. Related Releases

A select list of supplementary titles recorded during the years Postcard was active, many released posthumously.

1978

THE GO-BETWEENS – 'Lee Remick' b/w 'Karen'

Able, AB001

Pre-Postcard Australian debut single. The record which brought them to Alan's attention. 'Karen' was a particular favourite of Orange Juice.

1979

THE GO-BETWEENS – 'People Say' b/w 'Don't Let Him Come Back'

Able, AB004

Second pre-Postcard Australian single. Alan was a fan of the A-side but mourned the production 'which stopped it being great'. The lyrics for 'People Say' were later included in 1981's *Postcard Brochure* booklet.

JOSEF K – 'Chance Meeting' b/w 'Romance'

Absolute Records, ABS1

Pre-Postcard debut single on Steven Daly's label. A-side later rerecorded as Postcard 81-5.

FUN 4 – 'Singing In The Showers'
b/w 'Elevator Crash'/'By Products'
No Mean City, NMC010
Steven Daly's pre-Orange Juice vinyl debut as drummer with the renamed Backstabbers. Cover photography by Peter McArthur.

1980

THE FIRE ENGINES – 'Get Up And Use Me'
b/w 'Everything's Roses'
Codex Communications, CDX1
A Postcard that might have been. Alan was 'desperate' (says Edwyn) to sign the Fire Engines. They chose to release this debut themselves, funded by their manager. Future releases were on Pop Aural, the new label set up by Fast Product founder Bob Last.

1981

***VARIOUS ARTISTS* – C81**
Rough Tapes, Copy 001
Free cassette compilation available by mail order through the *NME.* The majority of acts featured were affiliated with Rough Trade, including a Postcard hat-trick: the single version of 'Blue Boy' by Orange Juice, 'Endless Soul' by Josef K from the unreleased *Sorry For Laughing* LP and an exclusive version of 'We Could Send Letters' by Aztec Camera recorded at Emblem Sound in Strathaven.

THE CLASH – 'Hitsville UK'

CBS, 9480

Of interest purely for the sleeve featuring a montage of independent labels, the Postcard kitten prominent to the right of the die-cut hole. Alan gave them permission to use the logo after Clash associate Kosmo Vinyl rang him up at 185. The song was guitarist Mick Jones's tribute to the post-punk independent label boom, its lyrics name-checking '*Factory*', '*Fast*', '*Small Wonder*' and '*Rough Trade*'. By coincidence, the title was Jones's twist on Motown's Detroit base Hitsville USA, echoing Postcard's ironic twist on Motown's 'The Sound of Young America' slogan, 'The Sound of Young Scotland'.

ARTICLE 58 – 'Event To Come'

b/w 'Echoes'/'Lost & Found'

Rational Records, RATE4

Bouncy single by Hamilton band released on Josef K manager Allan Campbell's label. The only non-Postcard release of the period to credit Alan Horne, here 'co-producer' with Malcolm Ross. Recorded at Emblem Sound, Strathaven (B-side 'Echoes' recorded by Wilf Smarties). Article 58's drummer was Steve Lironi, later to join Altered Images.

***VARIOUS ARTISTS* – The Fruit Of The Original Sin**

Les Disques du Crépuscule, TWI035

Double-vinyl Belgian compilation album. As well as the Orange Juice *Ostrich Churchyard* demo version of 'Three Cheers For Our Side', it includes the first recordings by Malcolm Fisher's project The French Impressionists: 'Boo Boo's Gone Mambo' and 'My Guardian Angel'. Both were arranged with help from Edwyn and recorded on a portastudio with Roddy Frame on guitar, Campbell Owens on bass and Paul Quinn on vocals. A deluxe CD was reissued by LTM Recordings in 2007 (LTMCD2497).

ORANGE JUICE – 'L.O.V.E. Love'

Polydor, POSP357 (b/w 'Intuition Told Me Pt. 2'), twelve-inch POSPX357 (+ 'Moscow')

Orange Juice's 'surprising' major label debut, a cover of Al Green's 1975 'L-O-V-E (Love)'. The seven- and twelve-inches have different sleeves. The latter's B-side, 'Moscow', is an alternative demo version from December 1979, notable for James's 'violin solo' in the middle eight. 'Intuition Told Me Pt. 2' included Edwyn's legendary lyrical homage to Baccara's 'Yes Sir, I Can Boogie'. Though not a Postcard release, both formats still feature the old cowboy-range typeface logo and drumming kitten mascot.

***VARIOUS ARTISTS* – Ghosts Of Christmas Past**

Les Disques du Crépuscule, TWI058

Festive compilation from Postcard's Belgium friends, includes the exclusive Aztec Camera track 'Hot Club Of Christ' – a Django Reinhardt-style instrumental medley of 'White Christmas', 'Away In A Manger', 'Have Yourself A Merry Little Christmas', 'God Rest Ye Merry Gentleman' and 'Jingle Bells'.

1982

ORANGE JUICE* – *'Felicity'

*Polydor, POSP386 (**b/w 'In A Nutshell'**),*
*twelve-inch POSP386 (+ **'You Old Eccentric'**)*

Their second major-label single in anticipation of the debut album. By the time of its release, James and Steven had left Orange Juice. The artwork still included the Postcard logo and kitten.

***ORANGE JUICE* – You Can't Hide Your Love Forever**

Side 1: *'Falling And Laughing', 'Untitled Melody', 'Wan Light', 'Tender Object', 'Dying Day', 'L.O.V.E. Love',*

Side 2: *'Intuition Told Me, Pt.1', 'Upwards And Onwards', 'Satellite City', 'Three Cheers For Our Side', 'Consolation Prize', 'Felicity', 'In A Nutshell'*

Polydor, POLS1057

Produced by Adam Kidron and funded by Rough Trade, the Orange Juice Postcard LP that would have been, first scheduled as 81-10. 'There's some diehards who don't believe that,' says Edwyn. 'They think it was financed by Polydor but it wasn't. It was financed by Rough Trade. I don't know if Geoff Travis still hasn't forgiven me because we kind of stabbed him in the back, really.'

'My attitude was, "Whatever!",' says Geoff. 'I just threw my hands up. I don't know if I was really, really upset or just half expected it. I think I was a bit shocked that Edwyn had done that. But it wasn't the end of the world. It wasn't, "Let's ring the lawyers!" That wasn't our way of doing things. It was more thinking, "Oh, these pranksters! How predictable!"'

Before Kidron, Alan had wanted John Fogerty to produce. He next considered Alex Chilton, formerly of Big Star: it was also rumoured in the press the album would include a cover of the latter's 'September Gurls'. As with their previous Polydor singles, the Postcard drumming kitten still appeared on the LP sleeve and disc labels.

The leaping dolphins cover was designed by future *Smash Hits* editor Steve Bush (the same magazine's Ian Cranna also managed the band), a late replacement for a standard group portrait by *Sounds* photographer Jill Furmanovsky which was scrapped due to the change in personnel between recording and release after James and Steven were sacked. Contemporary press adverts for the LP highlighted Orange Juice's new line-up, now consisting of Edwyn and David with Malcolm Ross on guitar and 'hip black drummer' Zeke Manyika.

The lyric inner featured a Harry Papadopoulos photo of Edwyn, Steven and David taken at BBC studios Maida Vale in October 1980 while recording their first John Peel session; the strange streaking effect is due to an accidental spillage which damaged the negative (the same image was later used for the cover of Domino's *Coals To Newcastle* box set).

The album title is a line borrowed from Jonathan Richman & The Modern Lovers' 'Hi Dear'; pedants will note Richman's original is actually 'you can't hide *that* love forever'. Working titles, whether real or merely intended to tease the press, included *Upwards And Onwards*, *Orange Juice 1* and the epic Biblical quotation *Love Is Patient And Kind; Love Is Not Jealous Or Boastful; It Is Not Arrogant Or Rude; Love Never Ends.*

The track 'Satellite City' was written about the Glasgow disco above the Apollo where The Nu-Sonics played in January 1978, the night Alan first saw them. The gig had originally been scheduled for a different discotheque on Sauchiehall Street. Had it not been changed, Orange Juice may well have written a song called 'Tiffany's' instead.

JOSEF K – 'The Missionary' (aka The Farewell Single)

Les Disques du Crépuscule, TWI053 (b/w 'One Angle'/'Second Angle')

Posthumous release of track recorded for Josef K's one proper John Peel BBC session in June 1981. The song's lyrics, by Paul, were inspired by Malcolm's father, who worked as a missionary in Africa. The B-sides were instrumental remixes of *The Only Fun In Town* album track 'The Angle'.

A CHA CHA AT THE OPERA – 'A Cha Cha At The Opera'

Island, WIP6835

The pet project of former child actor Joseph 'Joe' McKenna, of curiosity due to its genesis through Alan and Orange Juice at the time of Postcard (see pages 172–4). None were more gobsmacked than Alan that, more than a year on from that Hellfire Club rehearsal, McKenna managed to wangle himself a major deal with Island Records. And none were more annoyed than Edwyn that all music, though based upon Joe Tex's 'Ain't Gonna Bump No More (With No Big Fat Woman)', had been rerecorded and credited on the record to McKenna alone. In any case, the single flopped.

1983

ORANGE JUICE – The 'Felicity' Flexi Session
'Simply Thrilled Honey', 'Botswana', 'Time To Develop', 'Blue Boy'
Polydor, no catalogue number
Subtitled 'The Formative Years'. Free with early copies of the 'Rip It Up' single (Polydor, POSP547), a cassette-only bootleg of four tracks from Malcolm Ross's audience recording of Teviot Row, Edinburgh, 21 April 1979, same source as the I Wish I Was A Postcard 'Felicity' flexi.

1987

JOSEF K – 'Heaven Sent'
Supreme International Editions, EDITION 87-7
Posthumous twelve-inch single, taken from the same Peel session as 'The Missionary' (June 1981) and a contender for Josef K's best song. Paul Haig had since recorded his own solo version in 1984, while Malcolm Ross borrowed the riff for 'Turn Away', his contribution to Orange Juice's second album, *Rip It Up* (Polydor, 1982).

1992

***ORANGE JUICE* – Ostrich Churchyard**
'Louise Louise', '3 Cheers For Our Side'*, '(To Put It) In A Nutshell'*, 'Satellite City', 'Consolation Prize', 'Holiday Hymn', 'Intuition Told Me (Parts 1 & 2)', 'Wan Light', 'Dying

Day', 'Texas Fever (The Same Symphony)'*, 'Tender Object' *(*titles as listed)*
CD bonus tracks (John Peel BBC session October 1980): ***'Falling And Laughing', 'Lovesick', 'Poor Old Soul', 'You Old Eccentric'***
Postcard, DUBH922

Alan briefly resurrected Postcard in the early 1990s, augmenting a small roster of Paul Quinn And The Independent Group, Vic Godard and ex-Fire Engine Davy Henderson's The Nectarine No.9 with a couple of archive releases. The first was Orange Juice's mythical demo album recorded at Glasgow's Hellfire Club in May 1981, the best document of the original line-up in their prime (even with the purist-deflating organ overdubs of Primal Scream's Martin Duffy on 'In A Nutshell'). The beautifully packaged CD version added the band's debut Peel session. Limited vinyl editions came with an extra ten-inch 'Irritation Disc' comprising Alan and Edwyn discussing various aspects of Postcard's history over a strange instrumental backing.

'Holiday Hymn' was a Vic Godard song, arranged according to Alan's tape recording of Subway Sect's gig at the Music Machine, London, in February 1980. Alan later met Vic's manager, Bernie Rhodes, who took him to the legendary Rehearsal Rehearsals space of Clash fame under

Camden railway arches, where he gave him a typewritten lyric so Edwyn could learn the words properly. Orange Juice played the song regularly in 1981 during the last days of the original Postcard line-up. Godard didn't officially release his own version until 1985.

1993

***ORANGE JUICE* – The Heather's On Fire**
'Falling And Laughing', 'Moscow', 'Moscow Olympics', 'Blue Boy', 'Lovesick', 'Simply Thrilled Honey', 'Breakfast Time', 'Poor Old Soul', 'Poor Old Soul Pt. 2', 'Felicity', 'Upwards And Onwards', 'Dying Day', 'Holiday Hymn'
Postcard, DUBH932
The first official compilation of all four Postcard singles plus four tracks taken from period BBC sessions (Richard Skinner, January 1981 and John Peel, August 1981). The sumptuously packaged CD version included the hidden bonus of an early Nu-Sonics demo of Edwyn singing the New York Dolls' 'Who Are The Mystery Girls?'

ORANGE JUICE* – *'Blue Boy'
Postcard, DUBH934
Reissue of 1980 Postcard single to promote *The Heather's On Fire*. The four-track CD single included original A- and B-sides 'Blue Boy', 'Lovesick' plus the previously unreleased 'Poor

Old Soul (French Version)' and 'Poor Old Soul (Instrumental)'. An accompanying promo video was made using rare old Orange Juice cine film edited by Douglas Hart.

2000

JOSEF K – **Crazy To Exist (Live)**
LTM Recordings, LTMCD2319
Official bootleg of two concerts from Brussels, April 1981 and their last London show in August 1981. Includes the rare, late Josef K song 'Adoration' which they never had the chance to record properly.

2002

THE GO-BETWEENS – **Send Me A Lullaby**
Circus, FYL009
Double CD reissue of 1982 Rough Trade debut album. Of interest purely for the bonus disc including the first official CD release for both sides of their 1980 Postcard single, 'I Need Two Heads' and 'Stop Before You Say It'.

2003

JOSEF K – **The Sound Of Josef K (Live At Valentino's)**
Rhythm Of Life, ROL011
Released on Paul Haig's own label, compiling two separate gigs at the Edinburgh venue from

February and August 1981, alongside a 1979 TV Art demo of 'Romance'.

2005

***ORANGE JUICE* – The Glasgow School**

Domino, REWIGCD19

The ultimate Postcard-era Orange Juice compilation, squeezing all four single A- and B-sides plus the *Ostrich Churchyard* album on one disc with the exclusive bonus of 'Blokes On 45', their 'Stars On 45' medley pastiche recorded for the BBC's John Peel in August 1981. An added hidden extra is a 1977 Nu-Sonics demo of the Ramones' 'I Don't Care'. Sleeve notes by Steven Daly.

2006

***JOSEF K* – Entomology**

'Radio Drill Time', 'It's Kinda Funny', 'Final Request', 'Heads Watch', 'Drone', 'Sense Of Guilt', 'Citizens', 'Variation Of Scene', 'Endless Soul', 'Sorry For Laughing', 'Revelation', 'Chance Meeting', 'Pictures (Of Cindy)', 'Fun 'N' Frenzy', 'Crazy To Exist', 'Forever Drone', 'Heart Of Song', '16 Years', 'The Angle', 'Heaven Sent', 'The Missionary', 'Applebush'

Domino, REWIGCD30

Although not the first Josef K compilation – Supreme International Editions, Marina and LTM Recordings had previously issued similar titles – following the success of Orange Juice's *The Glasgow School*, Domino released this comprehensive best of. All four Postcard A-sides, selected B-sides, tracks from both the unreleased *Sorry For Laughing* and *The Only Fun In Town* and their one legitimate BBC Peel session (including the Alice Cooper cover 'Applebush' with vocals by Susan Buckley). Sleeve notes by Paul Morley.

2010

***ORANGE JUICE* – Coals To Newcastle**
Domino, REWIGCD38X
Epic box set featuring everything Orange Juice recorded spread over six CDs plus a DVD of promos, rare television and the 1985 *Dada With Juice* concert video. Its Postcard exclusives are the original live 'Felicity' flexi version, the four tracks from the related *Felicity Flexi Session* cassette and, for the first time, the complete BBC sessions. The latter disc includes three by the original line-up: John Peel, October 1980 ('Poor Old Soul', 'You Old Eccentric', 'Falling And Laughing', 'Lovesick'); Richard Skinner, January 1981 ('Upwards And Onwards', 'Wan Light', 'Felicity'); and John Peel, August 1981 ('Dying Day', 'Holiday Hymn', 'Three Cheers For Our Side', 'Blokes On 45'). Sleeve notes by this author.

2013

***JOSEF K* – The TV Art Demos**

LTM Recordings, LTMCD2549

A bonus disc of pre-Postcard rehearsal demos, exclusive to LTM's facsimile vinyl reissue of *Sorry For Laughing*.

***JAZZATEERS* – Rough 46**

Creeping Bent, BENT043

Vinyl reissue of self-titled 1983 *Jazzateers* Rough Trade album. Of Postcard interest purely for the four bonus digital download tracks available via a unique online access code with each purchase. Produced by Edwyn in 1981 for potential Postcard release, they feature the original Jazzateers line-up with Alison Gourlay on vocals: 'Stop Me From Being Alone', 'Love Is Around', 'Run Away', 'Moon Over Hawaii'.

***AZTEC CAMERA* – High Land, Hard Rain**

(Thirtieth anniversary reissue)

AED Records, AEDROD05

Commemorative vinyl edition of the Rough Trade 1983 debut album released with a bonus seven-inch EP. The latter includes the Postcard-era tracks 'We Could Send Letters' (*C81* version, recorded in Strathaven) and an exclusive bedroom demo of 'The Bugle Sounds Again'.

***ORANGE JUICE* – Thrillingly, Live At Stirling OJ 81**

AED Records, AEDCAS01

A bootleg cassette (and digital download code) of Orange Juice's gig at Stirling University on 10 April 1981 given away free with Christmas orders from Edwyn's AED label (www.aedrecords.com).

Pictures

All photo research and layout by Simon Goddard.

Back cover portrait: Edwyn and Alan in the summer of 1979 kindly supplied by and © Peter McArthur. (With thanks to Jill Bryson.)

Plate section: The Go-Betweens page 2, bottom left © Charlie Crawford (courtesy of Ken McCluskey); Edwyn page 6, Roddy page 7 bottom right, Alan page 8 © Francesco Mellina (www.francescomellina.com); Josef K page 3 top, Orange Juice with Alan pages 4–5 © Tom Sheehan (www.tomsheehan.co.uk); Alan page 1, Orange Juice page 2 top, Aztec Camera page 3 bottom, Josef K page 7 top © Paul Slattery.

The author greatly wishes to thank Tom, Paul, Francesco and Ken for taking the time to delve into their archives to provide these images.

Thanks

To Alan Horne and Edwyn Collins. Without whom, none of this.

And to all others interviewed for this book: James Kirk, David McClymont and Steven Daly of Orange Juice; Malcolm Ross, Paul Haig, Ron Torrance and David Weddell of Josef K; Roddy Frame and Campbell Owens of Aztec Camera; Robert Forster of The Go-Betweens; and to Keith Band, Jill Bryson, Clare Grogan, Gerry Hanley, Davy Henderson, Robert Hodgens, Peter McArthur, Gerry McNulty, Brian Taylor and Geoff Travis. Additional information and research material supplied by the Edwyn Collins archives/AED Records, Alan Horne, James Kirk, Malcolm Ross, Ken McCluskey, Douglas MacIntyre and Robert Sharp.

Very special thanks to Grace Maxwell for her endless hospitality, gossip, perspective and encouragement. Grace's own book *Falling And Laughing: The Restoration Of Edwyn Collins* is also published by Ebury.

To 'dear beginner' Phil King for kindly sharing his letter from Alan. And to that great Scot, and great friend, Tom Doyle for providing that last wee detail.

To my top cat Kevin Pocklington for banging the drum throughout, and to the big cats at Ebury.

With a purr to Holly Giblin for turning my scribble into a front cover.

And to my favourite Scottish person on the planet, Sylvia Patterson, who thought the original working title of this book was ‘hilarious’. Even if no one else did.

The Author

Simon Goddard first met Edwyn Collins in 1994 through their mutual fascination with sixties recording madman Joe Meek. He claims full responsibility for the failure of Edwyn's solo single 'If You Could Love Me' (because he directed the video) but only minimal credit for the success of the Orange Juice box set *Coals To Newcastle* (because he wrote the sleeve notes).

This is his fourth book about pop music. He lives in London.